Annie's recipes revolutionized our approach to the Daniel fast. The food was not only healthy but also flavorful, and this encouraged us to readjust many of our former eating habits after the fast was over.

—THE BAILEY FAMILY

The food is fantastic, and these meals are just perfect for me. Very yummy and fulfilling. I use these recipes often, without being on a fast. They should be used daily for good, healthy living.

—LAUREN LaDOTA

We absolutely love all of the simple yet healthy and delicious recipes that John and Ann Marie have prepared for our friends and family. We have tried many of the recipes and are thrilled at how easy they are to prepare. The meals are delicious and incredible, and they allow you to feel extremely satisfied but not too full. We plan to maintain the daily use of these recipes as a lifestyle; they are great during and after the Daniel fast.

—GREG AND CAROL MONROE

I can heartily say "Yum!" Good for the bones and good for the buds—taste buds, that is!

—DANA HARDEN HANKINS, ESQ.

I had the opportunity to taste the recipes that Pastor John and Annie put together for our church during the Daniel fast. I particularly love the salads. I was thinking they would not taste good, but to my surprise they did, and of course they were healthy. I thought you always had to soak your salads in heavy creamy salad dressing, but they taught me that olive oil, Braggs, and lemon dressing would do just fine. I also like cooking now with wheat- and gluten-free pasta! I thank them for putting these recipes together.

—CHIDI KALU

Annie's recipes always taste great. Her seasonings make the difference.

—Mom Cavazos

Ann Marie is a fabulous cook. Her food is so delicious that I had a hard time believing that it was made with ingredients that are usually associated with "tree huggers." She has converted me, and as a result I am both wiser and healthier.

—Pat Broussard, Esq.

THE DANIEL FAST

MADE DELICIOUS

JOHN AND ANN MARIE CAVAZOS

Library of Congress Cataloging-in-Publication Data
Cavazos, John.
  The Daniel fast made delicious / by John And Ann Marie Cavazos. -- 1st
ed.
    p. cm.
  ISBN 978-1-61638-180-6
 1. Vegetarianism. 2. Cooking (Fruit) 3. Nutrition. 4.
Cooking--Religious aspects--Christianity. 5. Fasting--Religious
aspects--Christianity. 6. Daniel (Biblical figure) 7. Cookbooks. I.
Cavazos, Ann Marie. II. Title.
  TX392.C38 2011
  613.2'62--dc22

                          2010038847

E-book ISBN: 978-1-61638-406-7

11 12 13 14 15 — 9 8 7 6 5 4 3 2
Printed in Canada

This book is dedicated to our daughters, Ariel Joy and Jerusha Leone, who have a destiny from God to fulfill. Their determination, tremendous work ethic, talent, beauty, plus God's anointing will no doubt take them where they need to go.

For the last ten years, all of these recipes at one time or another have been tried out on them with a resounding "thumbs up." Our time with our girls at home went so quickly, and now they are on the brink of being on their own.

Ladies, you are the light of our lives, and it has been a privilege and a challenge being your parents—we are very proud of you both.

Love, Mom and Dad

ACKNOWLEDGMENTS

WE WOULD LIKE to thank the following individuals for their support with this project: Hubie and Vicki Synn, Terry and Sandra Clifton, Karl Hudson, Jaimie Roberts, Dr. Mark and Ruth Chironna, Greg and Carol Monroe, Ana McDonald, Woodley Auguste, Jeanette Williams, Lin Parker, and Kevin Harris.

We would like to say a special thank-you to our wonderful photographer and friend, Catherine Harrover, who worked tirelessly photographing the many delicious Daniel dishes in this book.

And to all of our family and friends on whom we've experimented with these dishes—you ate healthy and didn't die! Thanks for being our lab rats! God bless all of you.

Finally, to our Lord and Savior, Jesus Christ: none of this would be possible without You. "Though one may be overpowered by another, two can withstand him. And a threefold cord is not quickly broken" (Eccles. 4:12, NKJV). We love You!

Contents

SECTION II: HEALTHY EATING AFTER THE DANIEL FAST

FOREWORD

ONE OF THE traditions that we have valued as a people at The Master's Touch International Church is our yearly time of fasting, prayer, and consecration to the Lord for those things that He desires to set in place within the context of our sphere and measure of rule. While we certainly make time for complete fasts, we have found that for the sake of our people and their busy schedules, the Daniel fast indeed serves and accomplishes the purposes of God as revealed in Scripture for an "acceptable fast."

The Daniel fast is taken from the life of the prophet Daniel, and you can read about it in the first chapter of the Book of Daniel, where Daniel requested that he not be defiled by eating the king's food and that he and his companions eat vegetables only and drink water for ten days. The commanding officer feared for his own life if Daniel and his companions looked like they were not thriving, as the king chose them to be amongst his choice leadership team. If you have read the story, you know the outcome. Daniel and the three Hebrew comrades looked healthier and fared much better than those who ate the king's food. The challenge with most fasts, including the Daniel fast, is that people find it difficult to maintain the discipline and the focus to be able to continue in obedience and faith for ten, twenty-one, thirty, or forty days before the Lord. That's just how it is.

However, with the right kind of planning, structure, and creativity, the Daniel fast can become a way to honor God, improve your own health and well-being, and even become the catalyst for changing your eating lifestyle for the rest of your life. The question is, How do you sustain a prolonged fast while not getting frustrated, bored, and fatigued? John and Annie Cavazos are multifaceted and multitalented, with rich resources and skills that enrich everyone they touch. Over the years it has been a privilege to have them both as friends and as colaborers in the ministry. While the demands on their life are extensive, and while they each carry a measure of rule in both the marketplace and the meeting place, they also have an incredible creativity when it comes to food and the directions of food.

What started with a few simple recipes for "surviving" the Daniel fast a number of years ago gradually became a wonderful compilation of nutritive-rich, vegetable-based dishes that were Daniel fast meals thoroughly acceptable on such a fast—and also thoroughly enjoyable. The recipes are so delicious that you could almost convince yourself you were eating everything at the "king's table" when, in fact, you are eating vegetables and grains only. John and Annie share a labor of love for healthy foods that are appealing to the pallet. This book of recipes, all original creations of this gifted couple, will go a long way to supporting you in pursuing God during seasons of fasting and prayer.

In addition, you will also discover that if you desire to change your eating habits so that your body can function at its highest and best, this cookbook can change your life and maybe even help you regain the health and vitality that the Lord wants you to have. Your body is the temple of the Holy Spirit, and as you already know, you are what you eat. John and Annie are gourmets in the kitchen, and they are extremely "temple conscious." They have distilled the best of their recipes that they have worked with over years of practice and refining and now are placing in your hands a special treasure that will become a great blessing to your own walk with God. These dishes are so tasty that even people who are so accustomed to the unhealthy, high-fat, high-sugar, American diet will find their cravings for unhealthy food dissipating as they allow live foods, living foods, to do their great work in keeping these temples in tip-top shape.

My thanks to John and Annie for their investment in the body of Christ and their willingness to share their creative cuisine secrets with all of us.

Happy fasting!

—Bishop Mark J. Chironna, MA, PhD
The Master's Touch International Church
Orlando, Florida

INTRODUCTION

DEAR FELLOW DANIEL Fasters:

This recipe book is not like anything else you've seen before. A recipe book for a fast—seems like an oxymoron, doesn't it? I mean, isn't the point of a fast *not* to eat? Well, in this case the Daniel fast is about *what* you can eat. The Daniel fast is a unique fast—taken from the biblical account in Daniel 1:8–21 where Daniel and his three Hebrew friends ate only vegetables and drank water for ten days. Our favorite part is verse 8, which reads, "But Daniel purposed in his heart that he would not defile himself with the portion of the king's delicacies…" This is indicative of the kind of man Daniel was—a man of purpose!

Our goal here is not to talk about fasting, per se, or give you tons of supporting scriptures. If you have prepared and purposed to fast, then you probably already know these things or have read about them in books far more poignant than ours. Rather, this book seeks to give you options, and more of them, as you embark on this unique fast known as the Daniel fast.

The incarnation of this recipe book began in response to our congregation complaining that they didn't know what else to eat besides lettuce and carrots when embarking on a Daniel fast. This told us that, number one, people didn't know much about vegetables, and number two, they probably didn't eat many vegetables! In addition, we found them spending more time bored with the lack of variety of food and less time focusing on why they were fasting. We decided to present recipes that would help them spend less time concerning themselves with what they shouldn't eat and more time deciding what they could prepare for their families. Thus, *The Daniel Fast Made Delicious* was birthed!

Back in 2004, during one of our Daniel fasts, we felt frustrated because we really wanted to see people enjoy the fast and benefit from eating fruits and vegetables. We were walking around a lake near our home when the Lord popped an idea into Ann Marie's spirit. She heard the word "Pumpkin Lasagna." She had no idea what that was, but the Lord told her He would show her how to prepare that and other healthy dishes using only vegetables and fruits.

A journey of learning began where we educated ourselves about vegetables— we shopped and prepared and ate things we never dreamed we would eat. We did a lot of experimenting—sometimes hit, sometimes miss—and we loved it, our kids loved it, and what's more, our family and friends loved it! We began preparing healthy dishes made only with vegetables and inviting our family and friends over to share in the fun. It quickly became apparent our signature dish would be Annie's Pumpkin Lasagna (chapter 2), since everyone loved it. The rest is history!

Now, the idea is not for you to eat more—you're on a fast, so you're supposed to eat less. Use these recipes to make the most of the food you *are* eating during your fast, but turn your plate down for one or two meals as you feel God leads— and only if your health permits. Please consult your doctor before making any changes to your diet.

The idea behind this recipe book is simply to educate you and to give you more healthy choices for you and your family as you embark on the Daniel fast. Those of you with spouses or family members who are not joining you on the fast will find this book invaluable. For those of you with children who are not fasting or who are picky eaters, there are some wonderful recipes in this book that will allow you to keep to the fast and also feed your family and not skip a beat when it comes to flavor! All of the Daniel fast recipes in Section 1 are wheat, gluten, and dairy free as well as vegan! In addition, the ingredients used in all of these recipes are organic—we encourage you to use organic whenever possible. If this is not possible, we encourage you to use a fruit and vegetable wash on all nonporous fruits and vegetables. Additionally, with all of these recipes we use cold pressed extra-virgin olive oil because studies have shown that olive oil offers protection against heart disease by controlling LDL (bad) cholesterol levels while raising HDL (good) levels. For further information, see www .healingdaily.com/detoxification-diet/olive-oil.htm. Why cold pressed? Coldpressed oil is produced with the use of a low heat technique, which keeps the flavor, nutritional value, and color of the oil. Although it is more expensive it is also of higher quality. For further information, see www.wisegeek.com/what-is-cold-pressed-oil.htm. One last comment: we like a lot of garlic and cilantro in our food, and our recipes reflect this. Feel free to adjust the amount of garlic or cilantro in any of the recipes in this book to suit your family's tastes.

People tend to think that to eat healthy means to eat yucky—not so. The secret is in how you season and prepare your food. These healthy recipes will not only show you different kinds of foods you might not have thought about before, but they also give you some great ideas on how to season and prepare your meals. It's all about choices, and the more informed you are, the more choices you'll have. After the fast is over, don't run out and get fast food! In Section 2 we have included dozens of healthy recipes so you can transition from the Daniel fast to making healthy eating a lifestyle! In addition, the pasta dishes are wheat and gluten free.

Medical studies now confirm that a large percentage of the health problems in America are digestive related. According to the website *Digestive System Disorders,* digestive issues for the most part cause a number of diseases, such as colon, rectal, and stomach cancer; diarrhea; diverticular disease; digestive tract gas; heartburn; hepatitis; inflammatory bowel disease; irritable bowel syndrome; lactose intolerance; and stomach and duodenal ulcers. According to a recent article written on digestive disorders:

> The function of the digestive system is to take the food and liquids that we put into our mouths and then either turn these foods and liquids into nutrients or energy needed by the cells of our body, or alternatively turn them into waste products that are then expelled by our body as bowel movements. When something goes wrong with this everyday process and some part of the process doesn't work properly, the end result is one kind or another of a digestive system disorder. There are many common digestive system disorders.[*]

---

* DigestiveSystemsDisorders.com, "Digestive System Disorders," www.digestivesystemdisorders.com (accessed September 2, 2010).

In fact, almost any natural health practitioner will tell you that food, good or bad, plays a definitive part in your health. The Daniel fast is a wonderful way to begin a life of good eating and good health. When we started doing the Daniel fast many years ago in our church, we started at the beginning of the year, around January 7, and for the next twenty-one days we consumed vegetables, fruit, and water—only! We did the fast for a number of reasons. First of all, turning your plate down and using that time to spend with the Lord is always a good thing. Second, after the holidays, most of us had abused food so much with all the celebrating we had done that we actually looked forward to the fast. Third, after a few years, a number of our members began to experience the benefit of the fast, because not only did we lose weight but also we felt better. Symptoms our bodies had manifested—such as heartburn, diarrhea, and irritable bowel syndrome—began to disappear. (NOTE: These recipes should never be used in place of physician-prescribed medications or medical procedures prescribed by your doctor for any and all medical conditions.)

Back in 1999, after we had moved from New York to Florida, our girls, who were six and eight at the time, seemed to always be getting colds, runny noses, ear infections—something anyone with children knows something about. I grew tired of taking them to the doctor every so often just to have the doctor give them another antibiotic. I was sharing my frustrations about this with our dear friend Ruth Chironna. She asked me if I gave our girls cow's milk. "Of course," I replied. "What else is there to give them?" She told me to get them off of it and introduce them to rice milk. I immediately began introducing a little bit of rice milk mixed in with cow's milk until I had weaned them off of dairy altogether. That was over a decade ago, and I can count on one hand the number of times in the last decade when they've been really sick or had really bad colds—and they never had another ear infection. They are now eighteen and twenty and are for the most part extremely healthy! This extended into our food, and before we knew it, we were eating better and going to the doctor a lot less. Do we ever cheat and have that slice of pizza or a burger? Sure! But everything in moderation! Changing our diet to include more vegetables, fruit, no sodas, and more water has significantly altered our lives. We trust that as you employ these changes, starting with the Daniel fast recipes, you will experience the kind of health that God intended for us to enjoy!

Whether you begin the Daniel fast at the beginning of the New Year or want to start it right now, we believe that *The Daniel Fast Made Delicious* is going to change the way you look at food, the way you prepare food, and the way you feel about food. Get started today! You're going to love these recipes!

What more can we say but…

Bon appétit!

Buen provecho!

Guten appetit!

HEALTHY EATING
ON THE DANIEL FAST

Chapter 1

BREAKFASTS

Jesus said to them, "Come and have breakfast."
—JOHN 21:12

Daniel's Fruit Fantasy

For a Daniel fast, we recommend that you drink 8–10 glasses of water each day and eat plenty of fresh fruit in the morning. For a quick breakfast on the run, choose two fruits from the following list along with a cup of tea or a decaffeinated grain beverage.

1 apple (all varieties)

1 kiwi

½ papaya

1 mango

1 cup red, green, or black grapes

1 orange or tangerine

1 pink grapefruit

1 cup berries (strawberries, raspberries, blueberries, blackberries)

1 peach

1 apricot

1 pear

1 plum

1 cup watermelon, diced

1 cup cantaloupe, diced

1 cup honeydew, diced

4–6 prunes

1 banana

AFTER-THE-FAST TIP

After the fast has ended, don't go back to the old junk foods and fast foods that got you in trouble in the first place. The After-the-Fast Tips throughout this book were designed to aid you in adapting these foods for a healthy lifestyle long after your designated fasting time is over.

CARING FOR BODY, SOUL, AND SPIRIT

During this special time of fasting remember to pray often throughout your day.

Fruit Salad *Serves 4–6*

1 cup strawberries	4–6 kiwi
1 cup raspberries	1 mango
1 cup blueberries	2 cups seedless red grapes
1 cup blackberries	1 papaya (see Appendix A, Tip #9)
2 oranges	2 cups diced watermelon
2 tangerines	4–8 mint leaves (optional)
1 pink grapefruit	1 lemon (optional)

Directions

1. Wash strawberries, raspberries, blueberries, and blackberries. Remove stems from strawberries, cut them in half, and add to a large bowl.

2. Peel oranges, tangerines, grapefruit, and kiwi. Cut away the flesh of the mango from the seed and thinly slice the mango lengthwise. Scoop the slices out of the peel and add them to bowl. (See "Peeling and Dicing Mangoes" under the recipe for Mango Chutney for more detailed instructions.)

3. Section oranges, tangerines, and grapefruit and add to the bowl. Cut grapes in half and add to bowl.

4. Cut kiwi crosswise and add to bowl.

5. Cut papaya in half, remove the black seeds, scoop out flesh, and add to bowl.

6. Add raspberries, blueberries, and blackberries to bowl.

7. Add diced watermelon to bowl, and mix all fruits together.

> ### AFTER-THE-FAST TIP
>
> Try adding this delicious glaze when serving your fruit salad after the Daniel fast.
>
> In a saucepan over high heat, combine 4 tablespoons of organic maple syrup, ½ cup water, lemon juice, and crushed mint. Bring ingredients to a boil, remove from heat, and let cool. After mixture has cooled, stir in 3–4 tablespoons of vanilla extract. Serve over the fruit.

> ### OPTIONAL MINT SAUCE
>
> Crush mint leaves and place in a separate bowl. Then cut lemon or lime in half, squeeze 2 tablespoons of lemon juice into the mint leaves, and mix well. Cover and let sit for 5 minutes. Serve over the fruit.

BREAKFAST JUICES

Note: We prefer that you don't peel any of the fruits or veggies in these juice recipes, since many of the nutrients are contained in the skin.

Carrot Juice *Serves 2*

2 large carrots
¼ inch ginger root
1 lemon
1 apple (any variety)

Directions

1. Wash carrots and ginger root.
2. Cut lemon in half or quarters.
3. Cut the apple in quarters.
4. Add all ingredients to juicer and juice.

Carrot and Veggie Juice *Serves 2*

2 carrots
4 stalks of celery
1 apple (any variety)
½ inch ginger root
1 lemon

Directions

1. Wash carrots, celery, apple, and ginger root.
2. Cut lemon in half or quarters.
3. Cut the apple in quarters.
4. Add all ingredients to juicer and juice.

JUICER RECOMMENDATION

You can make all of these delicious juices in a juicer. We recommend the Champion Juicer because it operates on the mastication process, chewing the fibers and breaking up the cells of vegetables and fruits. This gives you more fiber, enzymes, vitamins, and trace minerals. We find the juice is sweeter, is richer in color, and has more density. In addition, the Champion Juicer can also instantly transform into a homogenizer, which will allow you to make nut butters, ice cream, sherbets, and smoothies. For more information, visit their website at www.championjuicer.com.

Beet Juice *Serves 2*

2–3 beets
2 carrots
1 apple (any variety)

½ inch ginger root
½ lemon

Directions

1. Wash beets, carrots, apple, and ginger root, and cut in quarters.
2. Cut lemon in half.
3. Add the ingredients to juicer and juice.

Green Juice *Serves 2*

1 cucumber
4–6 stalks kale
½ bunch cilantro
4–6 stalks celery
1 apple (any variety)

4–6 stalks beet leaves
½ bunch parsley
1 lemon
¼ inch ginger root

Directions

1. Wash all the leaves and cut in half.
2. Add all ingredients to juicer and juice.

Vegetable Delight *Serves 2*

1 sweet potato, quartered
1 medium Vidalia onion, quartered
1 carrot
2 stalks celery
1 tomato
½ cup cilantro
1 scallion
6 stalks asparagus

½ cup parsley
1 cup green beans
1 zucchini, quartered
1 yellow squash
4 cloves garlic
1 tsp. lemon juice
Veggie or sea salt and ground black
    pepper to taste

Directions

1. Wash and quarter all vegetables. Add all ingredients to juicer and juice.
2. This can be served hot or cold. If served hot, simply microwave for 1–2 minutes after juicing is completed.

Chapter 2

MAIN COURSES AND COOKED SIDES

...so that I may finish my course...
—ACTS 20:24

Annie's Pumpkin Lasagna* *Serves 4–6*

2 lb. pumpkin (or calabaza squash)

Veggie or sea salt and ground black pepper to taste

¾ cup olive oil

4–6 ripe tomatoes

1 small sweet onion, chopped

½ cup leek, chopped

½ cup fennel, chopped

3–5 Tbsp. minced garlic

1 cup portobello mushrooms, sliced (or ½ cup baby bella mushrooms, sliced)

2–3 scallions (green onions), thinly sliced

½ cup cilantro, chopped

3–6 zucchini, thinly sliced lengthwise

1 tsp. tamari sauce

1 bag fresh spinach (or 2 10-oz. packages frozen chopped spinach, cooked according to package directions)

4 cups rice mozzarella cheese

1 cup rice Parmesan cheese

Directions

1. Prepare pumpkin base according to directions below and set aside.

2. Prepare sauce according to directions below and set aside.

3. Preheat oven to 350 degrees.

4. Spray 8 x 11 casserole dish with cooking spray or olive oil and set aside.

5. Heat 1 tablespoon olive oil and 1–2 tablespoons garlic in pan over high heat. Add zucchini to the pan and lightly brown. Remove pan from heat, but do not discard leftover oil. Remove zucchini from pan, sprinkle with salt, add tamari sauce, and set aside.

6. Add another tablespoon of olive oil and spinach to remaining garlic and oil in pan; return pan to heat. Cook spinach until tender, season with salt, and set aside.

7. Combine cheeses in one bowl.

8. Begin layering lasagna in casserole dish by spreading ½ of the cooked pumpkin to evenly cover the bottom of the dish. (Continued on next page.)

---

* This is our signature dish. We've included some time-saving shortcuts, but this entrée is best enjoyed when made from scratch.

9. Layer the remaining ingredients in the following order: ½ of the spinach, ⅓ of the sauce, ½ of the cheese, all of the zucchini, remaining pumpkin, remaining spinach, and ⅓ of the sauce.

10. Bake uncovered for 30 minutes or until the top or sides look slightly brown.

11. Top with remaining cheese. Bake a few minutes more, just until cheese is melted.

12. Let sit for 5 minutes. Serve with remaining tomato sauce if desired.

Directions for Pumpkin Base

1. Remove seeds from pumpkin (see Appendix A, Tip #1), wash, and place in boiling water or in microwave and cover with wet paper towel. Cook until fork-tender (see Appendix A, Tip #2).

2. Remove pumpkin from water and let cool for 10 minutes.

3. Remove skin or scoop out pumpkin and place in strainer and squeeze out excess water, then place cooked pumpkin in bowl.

4. Add salt, pepper, and 1–2 tablespoons olive oil to pumpkin and mix until paste consistency is formed. Set aside.

Directions for Sauce

1. Combine tomatoes, sweet onion, leek, and fennel in large bowl, cover tightly, and set aside.

2. In a pot, heat ½ cup olive oil over medium-high. Stir in 2–3 tablespoons garlic, salt, and pepper.

3. When garlic begins to turn slightly golden brown, add the mushrooms and sauté.

4. Add the tomato mixture and salt and pepper to taste, cover, and simmer for 10–15 minutes.

5. Stir in scallions and cilantro and let simmer on low heat for 5 minutes.

TIME-SAVING OPTIONS

- You can use canned pumpkin in place of the pumpkin base, but you should only use the canned pure pumpkin, not canned pumpkin pie filler, which has added spices that will not taste good with this recipe.
- Use prepared spaghetti sauce if you're pressed for time.

Spaghetti Squash Bowls *Serves 4*

1 spaghetti squash (the larger it is, the more it feeds, but the longer you'll have to cook it)
½ cup olive oil
4–6 Tbsp. minced garlic
1 sweet onion, cut in eighths
Veggie or sea salt and ground black pepper to taste

1 head organic broccoli
1 10-oz. package of frozen spinach (or fresh)
1 package portobello or baby bella mushrooms
½ cup cilantro (or other herbs)
1 cup rice mozzarella cheese

Directions

1. Preheat oven to 350 degrees.

2. Microwave squash for approximately 5–7 minutes or until fork-tender (see Appendix A, Tip #2).

3. Cut in half and scoop out seeds. Drain the squash on a paper towel and set aside.

4. With a fork, rake the meat out of the squash and place on a separate plate. Add 1 tablespoon of olive oil as well as salt and pepper and mix well. Place the squash back into the squash shell.

5. In a pot over medium-high heat, combine ½ cup olive oil, garlic, salt, and pepper. Sauté for 3 minutes or until garlic starts to turn slightly golden brown.

6. Add broccoli, spinach, mushrooms, and cilantro (or any other vegetable or herbs you like) to the pot and sauté for approximately 3 minutes. Add more salt and pepper if needed.

7. Spoon sautéed vegetables into the squash "bowls" and over the shredded squash and bake for 15 minutes or until slightly golden. Sprinkle with rice mozzarella cheese and return to oven for another 5–7 minutes or until cheese is slightly golden brown.

8. Serve with a salad or a couple of sliced tomatoes sprinkled with salt and pepper.

> ### OLIVE OIL RECOMMENDATION
>
> Throughout this book, whenever we reference olive oil in a recipe, we recommend you use cold-pressed extra-virgin olive oil.

Spaghetti Squash With Sauce and Parmesan *Serves 4–6*

1 spaghetti squash (the larger it is, the more it feeds, and the longer you'll have to cook it)
½ cup olive oil
4–6 Tbsp. minced garlic
1 sweet onion, chopped
(see Appendix A, Tip #8)

1 package of portobello or baby bella mushrooms, sliced
4–6 fresh tomatoes, chopped
Veggie or sea salt and ground black pepper to taste
2 Tbsp. organic maple syrup
2 cups rice Parmesan cheese

Directions

1. Microwave squash for approximately 5–7 minutes or until fork-tender (see Appendix A, Tip #2).

2. Cut squash in half, remove seeds, scoop out the meat, and place in bowl. Add 2 tablespoons olive oil. Stir until squash is evenly coated with oil, and set aside.

3. For the sauce, combine remaining olive oil, garlic, onion, mushrooms, tomatoes, salt, pepper, and syrup in a large pot. Simmer for at least 30 minutes.

4. Serve the spaghetti squash on plate, cover it with sauce, and sprinkle with cheese.

> **MAPLE SYRUP VS. HONEY**
>
> When it comes to sugar alternatives, both maple syrup and honey make great natural sweeteners. However, maple syrup has fewer calories and a higher concentration of minerals than honey. It contains the trace minerals manganese and zinc. Together they are important to the immune system.

> **QUICK FACTS ABOUT SPAGHETTI SQUASH**
>
> - Spaghetti squash weighs an average of 4 to 8 pounds.
> - Originally only available in pale yellow, an orange spaghetti squash called "Orangetti" was developed in the '90s. The orange variety is more common in grocery stores today.
> - High in beta-carotene, a 4-oz. serving of spaghetti squash contains only 37 calories.
> - Uncut squash can be stored at room temperature for about a month; cut squash can be covered and refrigerated for about two days; cooked squash can be packed in freezer bags and frozen.

Stuffed Eggplant Parmesan *Serves 4*

2–3 eggplants
2 Tbsp. kosher salt
½ cup scallions (green onions)
2–4 Tbsp. minced garlic
16 oz. ground tofu

1 32-oz. can tomato sauce
Veggie or sea salt and ground black
   pepper to taste
2 cups rice mozzarella cheese

Directions

1. Preheat oven to 350 degrees.

2. Place eggplants in large pot, adding 4–6 cups water (enough to cover the eggplants) and kosher salt. Bring to a boil.

3. Boil eggplants until fork-tender (see Appendix A, Tip #2). Remove eggplants from water and drain.

4. Cut eggplants in half lengthwise and use a spoon to gently scoop out the "meat" of the eggplants without breaking the skins. Set skins on a baking sheet to cool.

5. Place eggplant meat in a hot skillet with olive oil. Add green onions, garlic, tofu, and tomato sauce. Add salt and pepper to taste, and sauté for approximately 7–10 minutes, breaking up any large pieces of eggplant.

6. Spoon even amounts of the vegetable mixture into the eggplant skins on the baking sheet.

7. Place stuffed eggplants in the oven and bake about 30 minutes.

8. Sprinkle with mozzarella and return to oven for 5 minutes or until cheese is lightly golden brown.

9. Serve with salad.

Curried Eggplant and Cabbage *Serves 4–6*

3 eggplants
4 celery stalks
1 green cabbage
1 large sweet onion, quartered
½ cup olive oil

⅓ cup curry powder
Veggie or sea salt and ground black
    pepper to taste
1 tsp. cumin
4–6 Tbsp. minced garlic

Directions

1. Wash eggplants and celery, and cut both vegetables into bite-size pieces. (You can peel the eggplants or leave the peel on, depending on your preference.)

2. Cut cabbage in half, cut lengthwise into medium slices, and discard the core.

3. In a large bowl, combine eggplant, cabbage, celery, and onion. Set aside.

4. In a separate bowl, combine ¼ cup olive oil, ¼ cup curry powder, and salt and pepper to taste. Mix well and pour over the vegetables in large bowl. Stir until the vegetables are evenly coated with the curry mixture.

5. In a large pot over high heat, add the remaining oil and curry powder, along with the cumin and garlic. Stir until well blended.

6. Stir in the vegetables from the bowl, making sure all vegetables are evenly coated with curry. Cover and simmer for 7–10 minutes.

7. Test the eggplant pieces with a fork. If tender, reduce heat to low and let simmer for 7–10 minutes.

AFTER-THE-FAST TIP

After the Daniel fast, if you want thicker curry sauce, add 2 tablespoons of cornstarch to a cup of water. Stir until the powder dissolves completely, and add to the gravy in step #6. Stir and let cook for 5 minutes or until the gravy thickens.

Stir-Fried Eggplant *Serves 4*

2 eggplants
½ cup olive oil
4–6 Tbsp. minced garlic
1 large sweet onion, chopped
1 medium red onion, chopped
1 red bell pepper, sliced thinly lengthwise
4 stalks celery, chopped
4–6 ripe tomatoes, chopped

½ cup green olives, pitted
½ cup black olives, pitted
2 Tbsp. capers
2 Tbsp. pine nuts
¼ cup fresh basil, chopped
Veggie or sea salt and ground black
   pepper to taste

Directions

1. Wash eggplants, remove stems, and cut into 1-inch cubes. (You can peel the eggplants or leave the peel on, depending on your preference. It does not affect the taste either way.)

2. Heat ¼ cup olive oil and 2 tablespoons of garlic in a large skillet over high heat. Add eggplant and sauté until brown on all sides. Remove from stovetop and drain on paper towel.

3. Add remaining olive oil to skillet and let it heat over high heat. Add the remaining garlic and sauté until golden brown.

4. Add onions, bell pepper, celery, tomatoes, olives, capers, and pine nuts, and stir for 2–3 minutes. Simmer uncovered for 15 minutes or until sauce is thick, stirring occasionally.

5. Return eggplant to the skillet and combine with the other ingredients.

6. Remove from heat and stir in the basil just before serving.

> ### SERVE IT UP COLD OR HOT!
>
> This dish can be eaten cold or hot. If cold, let the dish cool, cover tightly, and refrigerate 2–4 hours or overnight. This is delicious over romaine lettuce.
>
> After the fast, it is delicious over any wheat- and gluten-free pasta.

Stewed Eggplant *Serves 6*

¼ cup olive oil
4–6 Tbsp. minced garlic
2–4 eggplants cut into 1-inch cubes
4–6 Tbsp. tamari sauce
1 large sweet onion, coarsely chopped
(see Appendix A, Tip #8)
1 medium red onion, coarsely chopped
1 red bell pepper, diced into ¼-inch
pieces
4–6 stalks celery, chopped

4–6 ripe tomatoes, chopped
2 cups zucchini, cut into ¼-inch pieces
Veggie or sea salt and ground black
pepper to taste
½ cup cilantro, finely chopped
½ cup scallions (green onion), finely
chopped

Directions

1. Heat olive oil and garlic in a large skillet over high heat. Add eggplant and sauté until brown on all sides.

2. Add tamari sauce, onions, bell pepper, celery, tomatoes, and zucchini. Add ½ cup water and stir all ingredients. Add salt and pepper to taste.

3. Bring to boil and simmer covered for 10–15 minutes.

4. Remove from heat. Sprinkle with cilantro and scallions and serve.

Serving Tips (During and After Your Daniel Fast)

During the fast this dish can be served over cooked green bananas, yams, yuca root, or sweet potatoes. These vegetables can be found in the produce section of your local supermarket or in an ethnic grocery store that features Hispanic foods.

After the Daniel fast, you can serve this delicious eggplant dish over brown or white rice.

Tamari Sauce

Instead of soy sauce, we use organic tamari sauce, and we particularly recommend a gluten-free tamari sauce by San-J. This product can be found at your local health food supermarket.

Curried Zucchini and Green Beans *Serves 4*

¼ cup olive oil
4 Tbsp. minced garlic
3 Tbsp. ground cumin
1 carrot, cut into thin strips
1 large sweet onion, cut in eighths (see Appendix A, Tip #8)
1 large red bell pepper, cut into thin strips

7 Tbsp. curry powder (more or less, to taste)
2–4 medium zucchini, cut into thin strips
¼ lb. green beans (fresh or frozen), ends removed
2 scallions (green onions), chopped
Veggie or sea salt and ground black pepper to taste

Directions

1. In a pot, combine olive oil, garlic, cumin, carrot, onion, and bell pepper, stirring all ingredients constantly so they do not stick to the bottom of the pan.

2. When vegetables begin to soften, stir in curry powder, zucchini, green beans, and scallions. Add a little more curry, if needed, and continue stirring constantly.

3. Stir in ½ cup water and bring to a boil. Stir and simmer uncovered for another 10 minutes. Add salt and pepper.

> ### SERVING TIPS (DURING AND AFTER YOUR DANIEL FAST)
>
> You can curry practically any vegetable. If you don't have zucchini on hand, try eggplant, squash, or calabaza. This dish can be served over cooked green bananas, sweet potatoes, yuca root, yams, or—after the Daniel fast—over rice or wheat- and gluten-free pasta.

4. Promptly remove from heat. Keep covered for approximately 5 minutes before serving.

Chili Con Tofu *Serves 4–6*

1 15-oz. can each of the following beans: adzuki, pink, red, pinto, and black beans
½ cup olive oil
5–8 Tbsp. minced garlic
2 Tbsp. cumin
¼ cup chili powder (or 4 Tbsp. chili oil)
16 oz. ground tofu (optional)
1 large sweet onion, chopped (see Appendix A, Tip #8)
5 celery stalks, chopped
½ cup fennel, chopped
1 cup leek, chopped
Veggie or sea salt and ground black pepper to taste
1 cup raw calabaza, finely chopped for garnishing (see Appendix A, Tip #1)
½ cup cilantro, finely chopped
4–6 scallions (green onions), finely chopped

Directions

1. Wash and drain all beans. Set aside.
2. Heat olive oil in pot over high heat. Add garlic, cumin, 4 tablespoons chili oil or ¼ cup chili powder, ground tofu, and beans, and stir until all ingredients are blended together.
3. Add onion, celery, fennel, and leek. Add salt and pepper to taste.
4. Reduce heat and simmer, covered, on low heat for about 1 hour.
5. Garnish with calabaza, cilantro, and scallions before serving.

Serving Tips (During and After Your Daniel Fast)

- If you have time, you can soak dry beans overnight and use those beans instead of the canned beans. Due to time constraints, we tend to use organic canned beans.
- After the fast you can prepare this dish with organic ground turkey or buffalo.
- After the fast you can serve this dish with millet bread (*Deland Bakery makes the best millet bread*) or sprouted bread, such as Ezekiel 4:9 Bread or Essene bread. (See chapter 12.)
- Add rice cheddar cheese along with the calabaza, cilantro, and green onions before serving. Serve it over brown, mahogany black, or jasmine rice.

Curried Cabbage and Calabaza *Serves 4–6*

2 lb. calabaza squash (or pumpkin)
½ cabbage head
2–3 sweet onions, quartered (see Appendix A, Tip #8)

½ cup olive oil
4–6 Tbsp. curry powder
2 Tbsp. cumin
6–8 Tbsp. minced garlic

Directions

1. Remove the seeds and rind from calabaza or pumpkin (see Appendix A, Tip #1) and cut into ¼-inch cubes or larger.

2. Rinse cabbage, slice into ¼-inch strips (do not shred), and discard the core.

3. In a large bowl combine calabaza, cabbage, and onions. Add ¼ cup olive oil and stir until veggies are evenly coated with oil. Add curry powder and mix the ingredients with your hands or a large spoon. Make sure that the veggies are completely covered with the curry powder.

4. Heat the remaining olive oil over high heat, and add cumin and garlic. Stir the ingredients around in the pot until the garlic is slightly golden brown.

5. Add the mixture in step #3 into the pot along with 1 cup water and cook until fork-tender (see Appendix A, Tip #2). Stir, then remove from heat. Cover tightly for 10 minutes.

Quick Tips

- We recommend Louisiana Hot Sauce because we like the taste. For more information, visit www.brucefoods.com.
- For step #3, you may want to wear plastic gloves to cover your hands because the curry powder has the tendency to stain. The stain is not permanent, but your hands might be left with a yellow tint for a while.
- After the Daniel fast, this dish could be served over jasmine or brown rice or peas and rice.

What Is a Calabaza?

We like to think of the calabaza as a pumpkin, but technically it is a round pumpkin-like squash. It varies in size—from as large as a watermelon to as small as a cantaloupe. Some calabazas are all one color—green, tan, red, or orange—while others are multicolored. Calabaza is popular in the Caribbean as well as Central and South America. It is also called a West Indian or Latin pumpkin. In the United Sates it is commonly found in ethnic grocery stores that feature Hispanic or West Indian foods.

Calabaza is similar in taste and texture to that of more familiar varieties of squash, such as butternut or acorn. You may substitute either of these more common varieties of squash for this recipe if you aren't able to find calabaza in your area.

Curried Tofu With Bok Choy and Squash *Serves 4*

2–3 zucchini, cubed
2–3 squashes, cubed
4–5 bok choy stalks, sliced
16 oz. extra firm tofu, cubed
½ cup olive oil
½ cup curry powder
1 Tbsp. cumin
2–6 Tbsp. minced garlic
1 sweet onion, cut into eighths (see
    Appendix A, Tip #8)

1 green pepper, sliced diagonally
2 tomatoes, chopped
½ tsp. crushed red pepper
Veggie or sea salt and ground black
    pepper to taste
Juice of 1 lemon
½ cup scallions (green onions), chopped
½ cup cilantro, chopped

Directions

1. Combine zucchini, squash, and bok choy in a large bowl and set aside.

2. Place tofu in a separate bowl. Stir in ¼ cup olive oil and ¼ cup curry powder until tofu is evenly coated with oil and curry.

3. Heat a large skillet over high heat. Add the remaining oil and curry powder, along with cumin and garlic. Stir until well combined. Then add in the onions, pepper, tomatoes and crushed red pepper.

4. Add zucchini mixture to skillet and stir until well combined. Add salt and pepper. Cover for 5 minutes.

5. Stir in lemon juice, scallions, cilantro, and tofu mixture from step #2 into the pot and cook for 5 minutes, covered. After 5 minutes, remove from heat and let sit, covered, for approximately 5 minutes before serving.

Broiled Stuffed Tomatoes With Basil and Pesto Sauce

Serves 4

2–3 large tomatoes, halved horizontally
½ cup frozen chopped spinach, thawed
1 cup rice mozzarella cheese
4–6 fresh basil leaves, chopped
2 Tbsp. pesto sauce (recipe in chapter 5)

½ cup cilantro, chopped
2 Tbsp. minced garlic
¼ cup rice Parmesan cheese

Directions

1. Set oven to broil.

2. Cut tomatoes in half horizontally. Scoop the meat of tomatoes out without breaking the skin and place "meat" in bowl.

3. Squeeze water out of spinach and place in the bowl with tomato meat. Add ½ cup rice mozzarella cheese, basil leaves, pesto sauce, cilantro, and garlic. Mix thoroughly.

4. Heat oil in pan over high heat. Transfer tomato mixture from bowl to pan and sauté over high heat 3–5 minutes.

5. Spoon mixture back into hollowed tomato skins, sprinkle with remaining mozzarella cheese and Parmesan cheese, place on baking sheet, and broil for 2–5 minutes.

FRESH OR PRE-MINCED GARLIC?

All of our recipes using garlic list "minced garlic" in the ingredients because we recommend the pre-minced garlic that comes jarred and marinated in oil. You can find organic varieties of this jarred garlic in stores like Whole Foods, which is what we prefer. If you prefer to use fresh garlic cloves, substitute 1 clove for every 2 teaspoons of minced garlic in these recipes.

WHAT IS RICE CHEESE?

Throughout this book, you'll notice that we recommend different varieties of cheese made from rice because they are a dairy-free alternative that you can enjoy while observing a Daniel fast. Rice cheese is available in many flavors and forms—block, sliced, shredded, and grated. One brand in particular with a wide selection of rice and rice vegan cheeses is Galaxy Nutritional Foods. For more information, visit www.galaxyfoods.com/Products/RiceCheese/.

Marinated Lemon Tofu With Cabbage *Serves 4*

16 oz. extra firm tofu
Juice of 2 lemons
4–6 Tbsp. minced garlic
½ cup olive oil
½ cup cilantro, finely chopped
½ cup scallions (green onions), finely chopped
½ tsp. crushed red pepper

Veggie or sea salt and ground black pepper to taste
1 tsp. saffron
½ cabbage, cored and cut into medium strips
½ cup Jerusalem artichokes, thinly sliced
½ cup carrots, shredded (reserve a small amount for garnish)

Directions

1. Cut tofu in small triangles. Place in bowl and set aside.

2. In a separate bowl, combine lemon juice, 2 tablespoons of garlic, ¼ cup olive oil, cilantro, scallions, crushed red pepper, salt, and pepper. Mix well and pour over tofu.

3. Cover tightly and set aside.

4. Heat remaining oil in a 1-quart pan over high heat. Add remaining garlic, saffron, cabbage, artichoke, salt, and pepper. Stir for 5–7 minutes or until fork-tender, not mushy (see Appendix A, Tip #2).

5. Add tofu and cook until tofu is heated through. Remove from heat and stir in shredded carrots.

6. Top with shredded carrots as a garnish and serve.

QUICK FACTS ABOUT SAFFRON

- Saffron's aroma and taste are often described as being similar to the sweetness of honey with hints of grassy or hay-like flavor.
- Saffron adds a luminous yellow color to foods.
- Saffron is widely used in Spanish, Arab, Indian, and Turkish dishes.
- Common saffron substitutes include safflower, which is sometimes sold as "Portuguese saffron," and turmeric.

Sautéed Veggies on Romaine Lettuce *Serves 4–6*

½ cup olive oil

1 Vidalia onion, cut in eighths (or 4 shallots, finely chopped)

4 Tbsp. minced garlic

½ cup fennel

Veggie or sea salt and ground black pepper to taste

1 bell pepper (any color), diced

2 yellow squashes, diced

3 zucchini, diced

½ cup leek, diced

1 cup broccoli florets

8–10 romaine lettuce leaves

Juice of 1 lemon

1 cup cilantro, chopped

1 tsp. tarragon

Directions

1. Heat olive oil in a pot over high heat. Add onions or shallots, garlic, fennel, salt, and pepper. Sauté over high heat until garlic gets lightly golden brown.

2. Add bell pepper, squashes, zucchini, leek, and broccoli, mixing until all veggies are evenly coated with the garlic and olive oil.

3. Season with additional salt and pepper if needed. Remove from heat. Add lemon juice, cilantro, and tarragon. Mix well, and cover for 7–10 minutes.

4. Serve on a bed of romaine lettuce leaves.

Stir-Fried Yellow Squash With Tofu *Serves 4*

2–3 Tbsp. minced garlic

1-inch piece of ginger, peeled and thinly sliced

4 Tbsp. vegetable broth

½ tsp. veggie or sea salt

½ cup olive oil

1–2 Tbsp. tamari sauce

2 Tbsp. Bragg Aminos Liquid

Juice of 1 lemon

3 yellow squashes, cubed

1 pack of firm tofu

2–3 portobello mushrooms (depending on size) or baby bellas, thinly sliced

1 large Vidalia onion, thinly sliced (see Appendix A, Tip #8)

1 large red bell pepper, seeded and thinly sliced

1 yellow bell pepper, seeded and thinly sliced

2–3 scallions (green onions), finely chopped

Veggie or sea salt to taste

Directions

1. In a bowl, combine 2 tablespoons garlic, ginger, vegetable broth, salt, 1 tablespoon olive oil, tamari sauce, Bragg Liquid Aminos, and lemon juice. Set aside.

2. Drizzle squash cubes with olive oil and set aside.

3. Drain tofu and pat dry with paper towel. Slice into 3-inch squares, half an inch thick. Cut each square into triangles.

4. Heat ¼ cup olive oil in deep pan or wok over high heat, rotating pan to coat evenly with oil. Place tofu triangles in one layer in the oil and fry until golden brown. Turn over and fry other side until golden brown. Remove from pan and set aside on a towel paper.

5. With the remaining oil stir-fry the squash, mushrooms, onion, and peppers for 3–5 minutes.

6. Add fried tofu to the pan, stirring gently. Pour garlic-ginger sauce over tofu mixture and stir gently. Cook for 1–2 minutes.

7. Remove from heat and set aside for 2 minutes. Garnish with scallions and serve immediately.

Broccoli, Shallot, and Sweet Onion Over Green Bananas

Serves 4

½ cup olive oil
5 Tbsp. minced garlic
1 head organic broccoli, chopped into
  spears
5–7 green bananas
3 shallots, chopped

3 tomatoes, chopped
2 medium/large sweet onions, chopped
  (see Appendix A, Tip #8)
Veggie or sea salt and ground black
  pepper to taste
½ cup rice Parmesan cheese

Directions

1. In a 4-quart pot, bring 4 cups salted water with ¼ cup olive oil and 1–2 tablespoons garlic to a boil.

2. As the water boils, add broccoli. When it turns dark green (less than a minute), promptly remove, drain, and set aside.

3. In a separate pot, heat 4–6 cups salted water. Add whole green bananas, with the peel on, and bring to a boil. When the banana skins split open, the bananas are cooked (approximately 20 minutes).

4. Drain and remove banana skins. Slice bananas lengthwise, remove the vein, and set aside.

5. Add the remaining olive oil, garlic, and shallots to a saucepan. Sauté over medium-high heat until the shallots get tender and the garlic is golden brown.

6. Add tomatoes and onion, and season with salt and pepper to taste. Cover and simmer for 5–7 minutes. Stir in broccoli.

7. Pour mixture over bananas and top with cheese to serve.

Cabbage Wraps With Sweet Potatoes *Serves 4*

¼ cup olive oil, plus 5 tablespoons
3 Tbsp. minced garlic
1 medium cabbage
1 bag chopped spinach
2 zucchini, cubed
1 small sweet onion, chopped (see
　　Appendix A, Tip #8)
½ cup scallions (green onions)
¼ cup leek, chopped

½ cup cilantro
¼ cup fennel, sliced
2–3 Tbsp. fresh dill, chopped
Veggie or sea salt and ground black
　　pepper to taste
2–3 sweet potatoes
1–2 Tbsp. cinnamon
½ tsp. nutmeg

Directions

1. In a 4-quart pot boil 3–4 cups salted water, adding 3–4 tablespoons olive oil and 1 tablespoon garlic.

2. As the water comes to a boil, peel 6–8 cabbage leaves gently off and rinse.

3. Use a pair of tongs to dip one leaf at a time in the boiling water. Hold each leaf for 1 minute on one side, then turn over and hold for 1 minute on the other side. Do this until the leaf is tender and pliable to the touch. Dip the remaining leaves one at a time and set each aside.

4. In a saucepan heat ¼ cup olive oil and remaining garlic. Add spinach, zucchini, onion, scallions, leek, cilantro, fennel, dill, salt, and pepper. Sauté for approximately 5 minutes. Remove from heat.

5. Take a cabbage leaf and fill it with spinach-zucchini mixture. Depending on the size of the leaf, you will use 1 or 2 tablespoons of the mixture per leaf.

6. As you fill each leaf, fold the leaves in and place the seams downward on the serving plate.

Sweet Potato Directions

1. Wash the skin of the sweet potatoes and cook in microwave until fork-tender (see Appendix A, Tip #2). Cut in half and scoop meat out. Place in a small bowl.

2. Mix cinnamon and nutmeg together. Mix remaining olive oil and cinnamon-nutmeg mixture with sweet potato and serve with cabbage wraps.

> **AFTER-THE-FAST TIP**
>
> After the Daniel fast, the cabbage can be stuffed with ground turkey and brown rice.

Squash and Brussels Sprout Medley *Serves 4*

2 carrots, sliced
1 cup brussels sprouts
½ cup olive oil
3–5 Tbsp. minced garlic
¼ cup water
4 yellow summer squashes, cut into ¼-inch cubes

3 shallots, thinly sliced
½ tsp. dried thyme
½ tsp. dried oregano
Veggie or sea salt and ground black pepper to taste

Directions

1. Sauté carrots and brussels sprouts in olive oil and garlic. over medium-high heat

2. Add ¼ cup water and continue cooking. When carrots get slightly tender, add the squash. Mix well.

3. Add remaining ingredients, along with salt and pepper to taste.

4. Remove from heat and cover. Mixture will continue to cook. Let it sit for 3–5 minutes before serving. Don't let it sit too long—you want the vegetables firm, not mushy.

Stuffed Zucchini With Sautéed Baby Bella Mushrooms

Serves 4

2–4 zucchini
2 scallions (green onions), chopped
1 large tomato, chopped
½ cup chopped spinach
¼ cup cilantro, chopped
½ cup olive oil
Veggie or sea salt and ground black
  pepper to taste

½ cup rice mozzarella cheese
3 Tbsp. minced garlic
1 package baby bella mushrooms, sliced
Juice of 1 lemon

Directions

1. Set oven to broil.

2. Cut zucchini in half lengthwise. With a spoon, scoop out the "meat," or the inside of the zucchini, and place in bowl. Place hollowed zucchini skins on baking dish and set aside.

3. Add scallions, tomato, spinach, and cilantro to bowl with zucchini and mix.

4. Heat ¼ cup olive oil in saucepan over high heat and sauté zucchini mixture for 2–3 minutes, seasoning with salt and pepper to taste. Break up any large pieces of zucchini in the pan.

5. Scoop zucchini mixture back into the zucchini skins and cover evenly with cheese.

6. Broil 1–2 minutes. Set aside.

7. In a saucepan heat remaining oil and garlic over high heat. Stir in mushrooms. Sprinkle with salt and pepper to taste.

8. Add lemon juice to the mushrooms while they are cooking. Serve alongside the stuffed zucchini and a salad.

Sautéed Kale and Spinach *Serves 4*

½ cup olive oil

1 large sweet onion, cut in eighths (see Appendix A, Tip #8)

½ cup leek, chopped

4 Tbsp. minced garlic

½ cup shado beni (or cilantro)

1 bunch fresh spinach

1 bunch kale

1 cup Jerusalem artichoke, sliced

Juice of ½ lemon

Directions

1. Heat oil in pan over high heat. Add onion, leek, garlic, and shado beni or cilantro. Sauté for approximately 2–3 minutes or until the garlic gets slightly golden brown.

2. Remove pan from heat and add spinach, kale, and artichoke. Mix all ingredients together until well blended.

3. Return to heat for approximately 2–3 minutes, remove immediately, and pour the lemon juice over the kale and spinach. Mix well and cover for 3 minutes, then serve.

> ### "I'll Take a Side of Pumpkin With That"
>
> This dish is delicious with a side of sliced pumpkin covered with cinnamon and Smart Balance Buttery Spread.

> ### What Is Shado Beni?
>
> Shado beni is similar to cilantro but has a stronger flavor. Look for it in ethnic grocery stores that feature Hispanic or West Indian foods. If not found, it is not a problem—just substitute with cilantro (add a little extra cilantro if you want the stronger flavor you would have gotten with the shado beni).

Sweet Potato Salad *Serves 4–6*

4–6 sweet potatoes

2–3 beets from small jar of whole beets (or about 1–2 fresh beets), diced

½ cup frozen peas and carrots

2–4 Tbsp. Vegenaise (mayo substitute)

Juice of 1 lemon

1 Tbsp. garlic

Veggie or sea salt and ground black pepper to taste

¼ cup scallions (green onions), finely sliced

Directions

1. Boil sweet potatoes in a pot with 4–6 cups salted water for approximately 30 minutes, depending on the size. Make sure the potatoes remain slightly undercooked. As soon as the potatoes are done, the pot should be removed from the stove. Drain and rinse sweet potatoes under cold water. Set aside and allow them to cool.

2. While potatoes are boiling, open the jar of beets and dice 2–3 (or see Appendix A, Tip #3 for instructions on using fresh beets). Place diced beets in large bowl.

3. Bring a small pot of salted water to a boil. Add frozen peas and carrots, and then remove from heat. Cover and let sit for approximately 5 minutes. Drain peas and carrots, rinse with cold water, and place in bowl with beets.

> **AFTER-THE-FAST TIP**
>
> After the Daniel fast you can use pickled beets for this recipe (from a jar, not a can). They add another dimension to the taste.

4. Once the sweet potatoes are cool, peel and cut them into medium quarters. Place the potatoes into bowl with beets, peas, and carrots.

5. Add Vegenaise, lemon juice, garlic, salt, and pepper. Mix well, cover tightly, and place in refrigerator for up to 2–4 hours before serving.

6. Garnish with scallions and serve.

Yellow Squash and Yam Salad *Serves 4*

3 yams, diced
½ cup frozen peas and carrots
3 Tbsp. Vegenaise (mayo substitute)
¼ cup scallions (green onions), finely
    sliced
¼ cup cilantro, chopped
1 small Vidalia onion, diced (see
    Appendix A, Tip #8)
Veggie or sea salt and ground black
    pepper to taste

¼ cup olive oil
2 Tbsp. minced garlic
½ tsp. cumin
½ tsp. medium or hot chili powder
½ tsp. turmeric
½ tsp. curry powder
2–4 yellow squashes, quartered
Juice of 1 lemon

Directions

1. Boil yams in a pot with 4–6 cups salted water for approximately 30 minutes (depending on size), making sure the yams remain slightly undercooked by testing with a fork. As soon as the fork can pierce through the skin, the pot should be removed from the stove. Drain the water and rinse yams under cold water. Set aside and allow them to cool.

2. While the yams are cooling, boil a small pot of cold salted water. When the water boils, add frozen peas and carrots, and remove from heat. Cover and let sit for approximately 5 minutes. Drain peas and carrots, rinse with cold water, and place in bowl.

3. Once the yams are cooled, peel off the skin and cut into quarters. Place the yams in a bowl with the peas and carrots. Add Vegenaise, scallions (leaving a little for garnish), cilantro (leaving a little for garnish), onions, and salt and pepper to taste.

4. Heat olive oil in a large skillet. Add garlic, cumin, chili powder, turmeric, and curry powder and stir until blended (about 20 seconds). Then add the squash and lemon juice. Stir and season with salt and pepper to taste. Cover and remove from heat. Set aside for 10 minutes. Garnish with the remaining cilantro.

5. Place the yams in the center of an 8-inch plate and surround them with the squash. Garnish with scallions and cilantro before serving.

6. This dish can be served hot or cold. If cold, refrigerate for approximately 20 minutes before serving.

Mashed Butternut Squash *Serves 4*

2 butternut squashes, halved
¼ cup olive oil
Veggie or sea salt and ground black pepper to taste

Directions

1. Boil squash in 4–6 cups salted water for approximately 30 minutes or until fork-tender (see Appendix A, Tip #2). Drain and let cool.

> **TIP**
>
> This dish can be eaten as is, or you can add rice mozzarella cheese.

2. Scoop squash "meat" into large bowl, add olive oil, and beat with a handheld mixer at low speed until smooth and fluffy.

3. Add salt and pepper and serve.

Mashed Calabaza *Serves 4*

2 lbs. calabaza squash, halved
¼ cup olive oil
2 Tbsp. cinnamon
¼ tsp. nutmeg
Veggie or sea salt and ground black pepper to taste

Directions

1. Scoop out any seeds and boil calabaza in 4–6 cups salted water for about 30 minutes or until fork-tender (see Appendix A, Tip #2). Drain and let cool.

2. Peel rind from the calabaza and discard. Place calabaza "meat" in a large bowl.

3. Add olive oil, cinnamon, and nutmeg. Beat with a handheld mixer at low speed until smooth and fluffy.

4. Season with salt and pepper and serve.

Mashed Sweet Potatoes *Serves 4*

4–6 sweet potatoes
¼ cup olive oil
2 Tbsp. cinnamon
¼ tsp. nutmeg
Veggie or sea salt and ground black pepper to taste

Directions

1. Boil sweet potatoes in 4–6 cups salted water for about 30 minutes. Test the tenderness of the potatoes with a fork. When tender, drain and let cool.

2. Peel potatoes and place in a large bowl.

3. Add olive oil, cinnamon, and nutmeg. Beat with a handheld mixer at low speed until smooth and fluffy.

4. Season with salt and pepper and serve.

Mashed Turnips or Rutabagas *Serves 4*

2 ½ lbs. turnips (or rutabagas), peeled and diced
4 Tbsp. olive oil
2 tsp. veggie or sea salt
1 tsp. pure maple syrup
¼ tsp. black pepper
1 Tbsp. parsley, chopped
¼ cup cilantro, chopped

Directions

1. In a pot, bring 3–4 cups cold water, salt, and turnips or rutabagas to a boil. Boil for approximately 30–45 minutes or until fork-tender (see Appendix A, Tip #2). Drain the water, let turnips cool, and remove the peel.

2. Add olive oil, salt, maple syrup, and pepper. Beat with a handheld mixer at low speed until smooth and fluffy.

3. Garnish with parsley and cilantro and serve.

Stuffed Sweet Potatoes *Serves 4*

2 large sweet potatoes
¼ cup olive oil
3 Tbsp. minced garlic
1 small onion, chopped (see Appendix A, Tip #8)
1 small green pepper, chopped
1 small red pepper, chopped
½ cup scallions (green onion), chopped

1 lb. ground tofu
Veggie or sea salt and ground black pepper to taste
½ cup rice mozzarella cheese
½ tsp. nutmeg (optional)
1 Tbsp. cinnamon (optional)

Directions

1. Preheat oven to 350 degrees.

2. Place the sweet potatoes on a microwavable plate and cover with a wet paper towel. Microwave until fork-tender. Once it is fork-tender (see Appendix A, Tip #2), cooking is complete. If not, continue cooking. Once potatoes are fork-tender, set aside to cool.

3. While potatoes are cooling, heat olive oil and garlic in a pot. Add onion, peppers, and scallions and sauté until slightly tender. Then add tofu and salt and pepper to taste.

4. When the potatoes are cooled, cut in half lengthwise and gently scoop out the flesh, keeping the potato skin intact.

5. Add the potato to the sautéed veggies. Mix well.

6. Spoon the sautéed veggie mixture back into the potato skins and place on baking dish.

7. Bake for 10–15 minutes or until the top looks brown.

8. Sprinkle with cheese and serve.

9. (Optional) Mix nutmeg and cinnamon together and sprinkle over the stuffed sweet potato before serving.

> ### AFTER-THE-FAST TIP
>
> After the Daniel fast you can add ground turkey or wheat- and gluten-free chicken sausage, finely chopped, to this recipe.

Sautéed Baby Spinach With Tofu and Tomatoes *Serves 4*

¼ cup olive oil
2–3 Tbsp. minced garlic
1 lb. firm tofu, diced
1 cup cherry tomatoes, halved
1 tsp. crushed red pepper
2 lbs. baby spinach, washed
2 Tbsp. tamari sauce

1 Tbsp. lemon juice, freshly squeezed
¼ cup scallions (green onions), sliced
¼ cup cilantro, chopped
1 tsp. dill
Veggie or sea salt and ground black
    pepper to taste

Directions

1. In a large skillet, heat olive oil over high heat. Add garlic, tofu, tomatoes, and crushed red pepper, mix well, and cook for approximately 5 minutes.

2. Add the spinach, tamari sauce, lemon juice, scallions, cilantro, and dill. Season with salt and pepper.

3. Sauté until the spinach is wilted. Remove pan from stovetop and serve immediately.

Roasted Stuffed Acorn Squash *Serves 4*

2 acorn squashes, halved and seeded
¼ cup olive oil
2 Tbsp. minced garlic
1 zucchini, cubed
1 yellow squash, cubed
½ cup baby bella mushrooms, chopped
¼ cup leek, chopped

1 cup fresh spinach, chopped
Veggie or sea salt and ground black
    pepper to taste
1 lb. ground tofu (optional)
¼ cup rice Parmesan cheese

Directions

1. Preheat oven to 400 degrees.

2. Brush the cut sides of the acorn squash with a tablespoon of olive oil and roast cut side down in shallow baking pan for 25–30 minutes (or until slightly tender).

3. In a saucepan, heat olive oil and garlic over high heat. Add zucchini, yellow squash, mushrooms, leek, spinach, salt, pepper, and ground tofu (if using). Sauté until the vegetables are slightly tender, stirring frequently.

4. Turn squashes cut side up in baking pan and spoon the sautéed mixture into the hollow centers of the squashes (where the seeds were removed).

5. Add a little water to the baking pan, return to oven, and bake for another 10–15 minutes.

6. Top with cheese and bake a few minutes more until cheese melts and serve.

Coconut Spinach and Okra With Yuca Root *Serves 6*

3 yuca roots, peeled
¼ cup olive oil
2–4 Tbsp. minced garlic
10-oz. package frozen chopped spinach (or fresh)

10-oz. package frozen okra
½ brick cream of coconut (not canned) (optional)
Veggie or sea salt and ground black pepper to taste

Directions

1. Boil yuca roots in 4–6 cups salted water for 20–30 minutes or until fork-tender (see Appendix A, Tip #2). Drain and let cool slightly.

2. While the yuca is boiling, heat olive oil and garlic in a saucepan. Add frozen spinach and okra, stir, and cover tightly for approximately 5 minutes. (Note: Don't let the oil get too hot before adding the frozen vegetables; it could splatter and cause a burn.). Then stir and cover for an additional 10 minutes.

3. Add the cream of coconut, salt, and pepper to the spinach mixture. Stir until well mixed.

4. Slice the yucas, pour the coconut spinach on top, and serve.

WHAT IS YUCA ROOT?

- Yuca root is a tropical vegetable grown in Asia, Africa, the Caribbean, and South America.
- Yuca root is high in starch and carbohydrates (almost 140 calories in an average size yuca root) and contains low levels of protein in the root and high protein levels in the leaves.
- Often prepared and served much like a potato, the yuca root contains much more fiber and slightly more potassium than a potato.
- When harvested, the root has a rough brown outer skin that covers a white, crisp textured flesh.
- Commonly used to make tapioca, pancakes, and snack chips, this root is also referred to as cassava root, manioc yuca, manioc, manihot, mandioca, and eddoes. It is often mistakenly referred to as yucca, which is a nonedible plant from the agave plant family.

Stir-Fried Edamame *Serves 4–6*

4–6 Tbsp. olive oil
1 Tbsp. minced garlic
¼ cup leek, thinly sliced
2 shallots, finely chopped
5–7 cherry tomatoes, halved

Veggie or sea salt and ground black pepper to taste
1 Tbsp. Bragg Liquid Aminos
1 Tbsp. tamari sauce
16-oz. frozen shelled edamame (or fresh)

Directions

1. Heat olive oil in skillet over high heat. Add garlic, leek, and shallots. Stir until garlic is golden brown.

2. Add tomatoes and salt and pepper to taste. Stir-fry over high heat.

3. Remove from heat and add Bragg Liquid Aminos, tamari sauce, and edamame. Mix well and cover for 5 minutes.

4. Add salt and pepper and serve with salad.

BRAGG LIQUID AMINOS

We recommend Bragg Liquid Aminos because it is a liquid protein concentrate derived from healthy soybeans and contains 16 amino acids. It is great on salads, soups, vegetables, tofu, rice, beans, and just about anything else you can think of. For more information, visit http://bragg .com/products/bragg-liquid -aminos-soy-alternative.html

Grilled Zucchini and Squash With Lemon and Cilantro

Serves 4–6

5–7 zucchini, diced

2–4 yellow squashes, diced

4 Tbsp. minced garlic

⅓ cup olive oil

Juice of 1 lemon

Veggie or sea salt and ground black
   pepper to taste

1 small sweet onion, finely chopped (see
   Appendix A, Tip #8)

½ cup cilantro, finely chopped

Directions

1. Place the zucchini and squash in large bowl. Add garlic, ¼ cup olive oil, and 1 tablespoon of lemon juice. Season with salt and pepper. Toss well, making sure that the zucchini and squash are mixed well. Cover tightly.

2. In a grill frying pan, heat the remaining olive oil over high heat. When the pan is heated, add the onion and cook for 2–3 minutes. Then place all the zucchini and squash in the grill pan and toss until golden brown.

3. Promptly remove grilled vegetables from heat and cover for 2–3 minutes. Then transfer to serving bowl. Add the cilantro and remaining lemon juice and mix.

4. Serve with salad.

Grilled Pesto Zucchini and Roasted Bell Peppers *Serves 4*

3 whole bell peppers (1 red, 1 yellow, 1 green)
2–3 zucchini, quartered
¾ cup olive oil
3 Tbsp. basil pesto (recipe in chapter 5)
Veggie or sea salt and ground black pepper to taste

Directions

1. Set oven on broil.

2. Place the peppers on a baking sheet and broil in oven until the skin is blackened. You may need to turn the peppers so all sides are evenly blackened. This procedure should take approximately 3–7 minutes. Remove peppers from the oven and let them cool for 5 minutes.

3. With a wet towel, peel away the pepper skins while they are still very warm. Cut peppers lengthwise and remove all seeds.

4. Combine peppers and zucchini in a bowl and mix with 2 tablespoons of olive oil. (If you are making the basil pesto recipe in chapter 5, add 1 tablespoon of minced garlic to the vegetables now.)

5. Prepare the basil pesto and combine 3 tablespoons of pesto with the zucchini and pepper mixture.

6. Grill the zucchini mixture in a grilling pan on the stove for 5–7 minutes.

7. Place the veggies on serving plates and add some pesto sauce on top.

TIME-SAVING OPTIONS

- We recommend Classico Traditional Basil Pesto Sauce & Spread if you don't have the time or ingredients to make your own pesto. This item can be found in the pasta and sauce section of your supermarket.
- As an additional time-saver, you can use 5–6 jarred roasted peppers (we recommend the Mancini brand) or purchase roasted peppers in the deli section of your supermarket.

Green Beans, Carrots, and Celery Medley *Serves 4*

¼ cup olive oil

2–3 tablespoons minced garlic

2–3 carrots, sliced diagonally

1 celery stalk, sliced diagonally

½ tsp. thyme

1 lb. green beans

1 cup baby bella mushrooms, sliced

¼ cup water

Veggie or sea salt and ground black pepper to taste

Directions

1. In a pot, heat olive oil over high heat. Add garlic and stir until slightly golden brown. Add carrots, cover, and cook for approximately 5 minutes.

2. Add celery, thyme, green beans, and mushrooms. Simmer uncovered, stirring constantly. Add ¼ cup water and cook for 5–7 minutes, stirring occasionally. When the vegetables are tender-crisp, remove from heat.

3. Add salt and pepper to taste, and serve.

> **AFTER-THE-FAST TIP**
>
> After your Daniel fast has concluded, you can serve this delicious veggie combo over rice- or gluten-free noodles.

Stir-Fried Vegetables *Serves 4*

¼ cup olive oil

4–6 Tbsp. minced garlic

½ cup red onion, diagonally sliced (see Appendix A, Tip #8)

1 sweet onion, diagonally sliced

½ cup portobello mushrooms, sliced

Veggie or sea salt to taste

2 cups fresh broccoli florets

2–4 zucchini, diagonally sliced

Juice of 1 lemon

Ground black pepper to taste

Directions

1. In a large skillet, heat olive oil over high heat and add garlic. Stir until garlic slightly turns golden brown.

2. Add both types of onion and mushrooms, and salt to taste. Stir constantly for approximately 5 minutes.

3. Add the broccoli and zucchini and continue to stir constantly for approximately 5–7 minutes.

4. Add lemon juice and salt and pepper to taste.

5. Remove from heat and let sit, covered, for 2–3 minutes or until crisp-tender.

6. Remove cover and serve.

> ### WHEN ARE VEGETABLES CRISP-TENDER?
>
> When we say "crisp-tender," we are referring to vegetables that have been cooked until they become slightly tender but still retain some of the crisp texture they had when they were raw.

Roasted Stuffed Bell Peppers *Serves 4*

½ cup olive oil
4 Tbsp. minced garlic
1 green pepper, halved and seeded
1 yellow pepper, halved and seeded
1 red pepper, halved and seeded
1 sweet onion, chopped (see Appendix A, Tip #8)
1 10-oz. package frozen spinach, thawed
1 zucchini, diced

1 turnip, diced
1 cup cilantro, finely chopped
4 tsp. chives, finely chopped
½ cup scallions (green onion), finely chopped
1 cup rice mozzarella cheese
Veggie or sea salt and ground black pepper to taste

Directions

1. Preheat oven to 400 degrees.

2. In a pot bring 4 cups salted water to boil. Add 2 tablespoons of olive oil and 1 tablespoon of garlic.

3. Using cooking tongs, place 2 pepper halves at a time in the boiling water and cook for 30 seconds. Remove and place cut side down on a paper towel to drain. Continue this process until all peppers have been placed on the paper towel. Drain water, transfer peppers to shallow baking dish, and set aside.

4. In a skillet over high heat, heat 6 tablespoons of olive oil and remaining garlic. Add onion, spinach, zucchini, and turnip. Cook until slightly tender, stirring constantly.

5. Remove from heat and add cilantro, chives, scallions, $^3/_4$ cup cheese, salt, and pepper.

6. Spoon mixture evenly into the pepper halves in the baking pan and place in the oven.

7. Bake for 10 minutes or until slightly brown. Sprinkle with remaining cheese and return to oven for a few more minutes or until cheese melts.

REUSING INGREDIENTS FOR ADDITIONAL RECIPES

If we are preparing Eggplant Parmesan (see recipe earlier in this chapter), we use any leftover ingredients either to stuff zucchini or bell peppers like the ones in this recipe.

Stir-Fried Broccoli and Cabbage *Serves 4*

½ cup olive oil
4 Tbsp. minced garlic
½ cabbage, cored and shredded
4 Tbsp. tamari sauce

1 head broccoli, cut into spears
Veggie or sea salt and ground black
pepper to taste

Directions

1. In a large pot or wok, heat olive oil over high heat, and then add garlic and cabbage, stirring constantly.

2. Add tamari sauce and broccoli; stir-fry until the broccoli turns a bright green and cabbage and broccoli are tender-crisp.

3. Remove from heat, sprinkle with salt and pepper, and serve.

WHY CABBAGE AND BROCCOLI?

In preparing this dish, you could add tofu or shredded carrots. However, we like combining the broccoli and cabbage together when we are stir-frying or cooking because not only does it taste good, but also in our research we discovered that cabbage, which is sorely misunderstood in this country, is highly beneficial. Cabbage contains indoles, and current research indicates that indoles can lower the risk of various forms of cancer. Epidemiological studies have found that men living in China and Japan (where cabbage abounds) experience a much lower rate of prostate cancer than their American counterparts. Similar data have been uncovered regarding breast cancer rates among women. Cabbage is rich in the following nutrients: vitamin A, vitamin C, vitamin E, and vitamin B.

The health benefits of eating broccoli are as follows: It provides high amounts of vitamin C, which aids iron absorption in the body. It prevents the development of cataracts and also eases the symptoms of the common cold. It also aids those battling high blood pressure, while a large amount of calcium helps combat osteoporosis. Broccoli is also fiber-rich, which enhances the gastrointestinal (GI) tract as well as aims to reduce blood cholesterol levels. Additionally, the health benefits of broccoli have been linked to preventing and controlling the following medical concerns: Alzheimer's disease, diabetes, calcium deficiencies, stomach and colon cancer, malignant tumors, lung cancer, heart disease, arthritis, and even the aging process.

Ginger Tofu With Asparagus *Serves 6*

1 lb. asparagus
¼ cup olive oil
3 Tbsp. minced garlic
2 tsp. minced ginger
1 lb. firm tofu, diced

2 Tbsp. tamari sauce
Juice of 2 limes
Veggie or sea salt and ground black
 pepper to taste

Directions

1. Wash the asparagus and cut off the ends (¼ inch).
2. In a large skillet, heat olive oil over high heat. Add the garlic and ginger, stirring until the garlic is slightly golden.
3. Add the tofu, tamari, and asparagus. Mix and cover for 5 minutes.
4. Remove from stove. Add lime juice and salt and pepper to taste.
5. Let sit, covered, for another 5–7 minutes before serving.

Steamed Brussels Sprouts With Garlic *Serves 4*

½ cup olive oil
4 Tbsp. garlic
1 carton fresh brussels sprouts
2–3 shallots, finely chopped

1 Tbsp. lemon juice
Veggie or sea salt and ground black
 pepper to taste

Directions

1. In a pot, add 2 tablespoons olive oil and 1 tablespoon of garlic to salted water and bring to a boil.
2. While water is heating, remove any yellow leaves and trim the stems of the sprouts. With a sharp knife cut an X into stem end of each sprout. Rinse the sprouts and set aside.
3. In a pan, add 3 tablespoons of olive oil and remaining garlic and sauté the shallots until slightly golden brown. Remove from heat and let cool.
4. In a bowl, mix lemon juice, shallots, salt, pepper, and remaining olive oil. Set aside.
5. Toss brussels sprouts in boiling water for 30 seconds or until fork-tender (see Appendix A, Tip #2).
6. Drain sprouts, transfer to a serving bowl, and cover with the lemon juice mixture. Stir the sprouts until evenly coated. Add salt and pepper to taste.
7. Let sit, covered, for 5 minutes before serving.

Daniel's Vegetable Shepherd's Pie *Serves 4–6*

3 yams or sweet potatoes

1 cup frozen peas and carrots

1–2 cups frozen green beans, cut

½ cup hemp milk

¼ cup olive oil

2–3 Tbsp. minced garlic

1 tsp. cumin

1 lb. ground tofu

2 tomatoes

Veggie or sea salt and ground black pepper to taste

2–4 cups rice cheddar cheese

Directions

1. Preheat oven to 375 degrees.

2. Boil yams in 4–6 cups salted water for 30 minutes or until fork-tender (see Appendix A, Tip #2), whichever comes first. Remove from heat, drain, and set aside to cool.

3. In a separate pot boil 4 cups salted water. Add the frozen peas, carrots, and green beans to boiling water. Stir and remove from heat. Let the pot sit, covered, for 5–7 minutes. Then drain.

4. When yams are cool, peel and discard skin and mash with a potato masher. Add milk and wisk or use a hand-held mixer to continue mashing.

5. In a pan over high heat, combine olive oil, garlic, and cumin. Stir in tofu, tomatoes, peas, carrots, and green beans until well mixed. Sprinkle with salt and pepper.

6. Spray a 2-quart casserole dish with olive oil cooking spray. Spread half of the mashed yams in an even layer across the bottom of the dish. Then spread a layer of half of the veggies and a layer of half of the cheese. Repeat the three layers, using up the remaining ingredients for each layer.

7. Bake until the cheesy top layer develops a light brown crust. Cool slightly before serving.

Stuffed Mushrooms *Serves 4–6*

12 large white mushrooms
1 Tbsp. minced garlic
1 Tbsp. onion, minced
1 yellow squash, finely diced
1 tsp. lemon juice

½ cup Vegenaise (mayo substitute)
3 Tbsp. rice Parmesan cheese
Veggie or sea salt and black pepper to taste

Directions

1. Preheat oven to 325 degrees.

2. Wash mushrooms and pat dry with a towel. Remove and finely chop the mushroom stems. Reserve chopped stems.

3. Place the mushroom caps on a baking sheet, rounded side up.

4. Sauté garlic, onion, squash, and mushroom stems for 10 minutes. Then add the lemon juice.

5. Remove from pan and put in a bowl. Add Vegenaise and cheese to the cooked mixture and mix.

6. Stuff each mushroom cap with the ingredients by evenly spooning the squash mixture into each mushroom.

7. Place the stuffed mushrooms in the oven for another 10–15 minutes or until lightly browned (depending on oven temperature).

> **FOLLOW YOUR HEART**
>
> Follow Your Heart is a company that produces egg-free, diary-free mayonnaise substitutes such as Vegenaise (mayo substitute). Their products contain no cholesterol, no preservatives, and no genetically modified foods (GMs).

> **WHAT IS VEGENAISE?**
>
> Vegenaise (mayo substitute) is egg free, dairy free, and contains no cholesterol and no preservatives. We use this product practically in everything that requires mayonnaise. It gives added substance and is the perfect healthy substitute for mayonnaise. Our kids don't even know the difference! This product can be purchased at health food stores or local supermarkets that have organic/health food aisles or sections.

Spicy Grilled Vegetables *Serves 4*

2 large zucchini, cut into medium-size
   pieces
1 red bell pepper, cut into medium-size
   pieces
1 yellow bell pepper, cut into medium-
   size pieces
1 large Spanish onion, cut into medium-
   size pieces
   (see Appendix A, Tip #8)
1 medium sweet onion, cut into medium-
   size pieces
1 eggplant, cut into medium-size pieces
½ cup olive oil

Juice of ½ lemon
½ cup cilantro, chopped
3–5 Tbsp. minced garlic
1 Tbsp. chili powder
½ tsp. oregano
½ tsp. thyme
½ tsp. cayenne pepper
1 Tbsp. Braggs Liquid Aminos
2 Tbsp. tamari sauce
Veggie or sea salt and ground black
   pepper to taste

Directions

1. Place first six ingredients in a large bowl.

2. To prepare marinade, in a separate bowl combine olive oil, lemon juice, cilantro, garlic, chili powder, oregano, thyme, cayenne pepper, Braggs Liquid Aminos, tamari sauce, salt, and pepper.

3. Add marinade to vegetables and mix thoroughly until the vegetables are evenly coated. Cover and marinate for 1 hour.

4. Spray a grill pan (see Appendix A, Tip #4) with cooking spray before heating. Place the vegetables on the hot grill. Leftover marinade sauce can be applied to the vegetables with a brush while they are grilling. Continue the process until all the veggies are golden brown on both sides.

5. Serve with a small salad.

Roasted Cauliflower With Cranberry *Serves 4–6*

1 head cauliflower
½ cup dried cranberries
1 Tbsp. lemon juice
3 Tbsp. minced garlic

¼ cup olive oil
Veggie or sea salt and ground black
   pepper to taste

Directions

1. Preheat oven to 425 degrees.

2. Wash and section the cauliflower into florets and place in large bowl.

3. Place the cranberries in a small bowl and cover with hot water. In another bowl mix together 1 tablespoon of lemon juice, garlic, olive oil, salt, and pepper.

4. Coat florets with the mixture. Spoon cauliflower into a baking dish.

5. Place baking dish in the center of the oven and bake for approximately 10–15 minutes or until the cauliflower is brown and tender.

6. Drain the cranberries and sprinkle them over the cauliflower and serve.

Parmesan Asparagus *Serves 4*

3 Tbsp. minced garlic
½ cup olive oil
½ cup rice Parmesan cheese
Veggie or sea salt and ground black
   pepper to taste

1 bunch asparagus
Juice of 1 lemon
3 Tbsp. cilantro

> **SERVING RECOMMENDATION**
>
> We recommend serving the two dishes on this page together!

Directions

1. Preheat oven to 425 degrees.

2. Boil 4 cups salted water, adding 1 tablespoon of garlic and 2 tablespoons of olive oil to the water.

3. In a small bowl combine the remaining garlic and olive oil, cheese, salt, and pepper.

4. Place the asparagus in boiling water for 30 seconds. Remove promptly and place on baking dish.

5. Coat asparagus with the cheese mixture and bake for 5–7 minutes.

6. After removing from the oven, sprinkle lemon juice, cilantro, and Parmesan cheese over the asparagus.

Pars-n-Turns Stir-Fry *Serves 4*

¼ cup olive oil
4 Tbsp. minced garlic
½ tsp. cumin
½ tsp. dried thyme
½ cup shado beni
½ cup parsnips, peeled and sliced
½ cup turnips, peeled and sliced
1 red onion, halved and sliced (see Appendix A, Tip #8)
1 red bell pepper, sliced

Veggie or sea salt and ground black pepper to taste
½ cup french green beans
½ cup green peas
½ cup cilantro, chopped
½ cup scallions (green onions), chopped
Juice of 1 lemon
1 tsp. dill

Directions

1. In a medium saucepan heat olive oil over high heat. Add garlic, cumin, thyme, shado beni, parsnips, turnips, onion, and bell pepper. Add salt and pepper and stir-fry for 3–5 minutes.

2. Cover for 5–7 minutes or until parsnips and turnips are fork-tender (see Appendix A, Tip #2). You may want to add 2–3 tablespoons of water to aid in cooking the Pars-N-Turns.

3. Add the green beans, peas, cilantro, and scallions, and mix well. Cover; let sit for 2–5 minutes.

4. Stir in lemon juice, dill, salt, and pepper.

5. Remove from heat and let sit, covered, for another 2 minutes. Add additional seasoning according to taste before serving.

Stir-Fried Rutabaga, Kale, and Beet *Serves 4*

2 cups rutabaga leaves
2 cups rainbow kale (or green kale)
2 cups beet leaves
½ cup olive oil
4 Tbsp. minced garlic
1 sweet onion, diagonally cut (see
    Appendix A, Tip #8)

½ cup leek, thinly sliced
½ cup fennel, thinly sliced
4 Tbsp. tamari sauce
½ tsp. dried thyme
Veggie or sea salt and ground black
    pepper to taste
1–2 Tbsp. lemon juice

Directions

1. Wash rutabaga leaves, kale, and beet leaves, and chop coarsely.

2. In a pot over high heat, heat olive oil. Add garlic, onion, leek, and fennel. Stir-fry until the ingredients are lightly golden brown.

3. Toss the rutabaga, kale, and beets into the pot and mix well. Add tamari sauce, thyme, and salt and pepper to taste; cover, and cook for approximately 3–5 minutes. After 5 minutes remove cover and stir. Make sure vegetables are tender-crisp.

4. Remove pot from stove. Add lemon juice and mix well. Cover for another 5 minutes before serving.

Roasted Yams With Cilantro *Serves 4–6*

½ cup olive oil
½ cup cilantro
½ tsp. dried thyme
2 Tbsp. cayenne or Cajun spice

Veggie or sea salt to taste
Black pepper to taste
4–6 medium yams, peeled and quartered

Directions

1. Preheat oven to 375 degrees.

2. Combine ¼ cup olive oil, cilantro (leave 2 tablespoons for garnishing), thyme, cayenne or Cajun spice, salt, and pepper. Add yams and stir until yams are fully coated.

3. Spread remaining oil over a baking sheet. Place yams on the baking sheet and bake for approximately 1 hour. You may want to check the yams periodically and turn them over halfway through baking.

4. When the yams are fork-tender (see Appendix A, Tip #2), remove from oven and sprinkle the remaining cilantro over yams. Enjoy with a green salad.

Mashed Winter Root Casserole
With Crispy Onion Topping *Serves 8*

7 cups vegetable broth
3 lbs. sweet potatoes, peeled and cubed
1½ lbs. rutabagas, peeled and cubed
1¼ lbs. parsnips, peeled and cubed
4 Tbsp. minced garlic
1 bay leaf
1 tsp. dried thyme

¾ cup rice or hemp milk
Veggie or sea salt and ground black
    pepper to taste
¼ cup olive oil
3 onions, thinly sliced
    (see Appendix A, Tip #8)

Directions

1. Preheat oven to 375 degrees.

2. In a large pot over high heat, combine broth, sweet potatoes, rutabagas, parsnips, garlic, bay leaf, and thyme. As soon as mixture boils, reduce heat and cover. Simmer until very tender, about 30 minutes. Drain and remove the bay leaf.

3. Transfer vegetables to a large bowl. Add milk, salt, and pepper. Use a handheld electric mixer to mash mixture to desired consistency. Transfer to a baking dish.

4. Heat olive oil in a skillet over medium-high heat. Add onions and sauté until golden brown. Sprinkle with salt and pepper. Spread onions evenly over mashed vegetables.

5. Bake, uncovered, for 25 minutes or until onion topping becomes crispy.

TIME-SAVING TIPS

- The smaller you make the pieces when cutting your vegetables into cubes, the faster they will become tender in step 2.
- This dish can be prepared up to one day in advance. After step 4, simply cover the unbaked casserole and refrigerate. Add a few extra minutes of baking time since the casserole will be cold when you put it in the oven the next day.

Shredded Vegetables and Spaghetti Squash *Serves 4*

1 spaghetti squash cut in half
½ cup olive oil
1 sweet onion, chopped (see Appendix A, Tip #8)
4–6 Tbsp. minced garlic
1 small red cabbage, shredded

4–6 tomatoes, chopped
1 zucchini, shredded lengthwise
¼ cup fresh basil
1 Tbsp. dry oregano
Veggie or sea salt and ground black pepper to taste

Directions

1. Cover spaghetti squash with a wet paper towel and microwave on high until fork-tender (see Appendix A, Tip #2), approximately 5–6 minutes (microwave cooking times may vary).

2. Let cool slightly and remove the seeds from each half. Then use a fork to "rake" the flesh out of the squash, creating strands that resemble spaghetti.

3. In a pan over high heat, heat olive oil and sauté the onion, garlic, and cabbage for approximately 20 minutes or until the cabbage is fork-tender, whichever comes first.

4. Then add tomatoes, zucchini, basil, oregano, salt, and pepper. Simmer for approximately 3 minutes. Then let stand covered for 5 minutes.

5. Remove from heat and add the spaghetti squash and mix thoroughly. Add more salt or pepper to taste if needed before serving.

Parslied Zucchini and Broccoli *Serves 4*

1½ cups vegetable broth
4–6 Tbsp. minced garlic
4–6 zucchini, cubed
1 cup broccoli florets
¼ cup olive oil
1 sweet onion, chopped (see Appendix
    A, Tip #8)

Veggie or sea salt and ground black
    pepper to taste
1 cup fresh parsley, chopped
½ cup cilantro, chopped

Directions

1. Bring vegetable broth to a boil and add 1 tablespoon of garlic. Place the zucchini in a colander or wok strainer and dip into boiling water for no more than 5–10 seconds. Remove zucchini from broth, drain, and place in a bowl.

2. Repeat step 1 with the broccoli florets. Add the broccoli to the bowl of zucchini and set aside.

3. Heat olive oil in a skillet over high heat. Sauté the onions and remaining garlic until tender.

4. Add salt and pepper to taste, and ¾ cup of the parsley to the skillet. Mix well and simmer for 2 minutes.

5. Pour the sauce over the zucchini and broccoli. Sprinkle with the cilantro and remaining parsley and serve.

Shredded Zucchini (Spaghetti) and Tomato Sauce *Serves 4*

2–4 zucchini, shredded

¼ cup olive oil

2 Tbsp. minced garlic

1 cup portobello mushrooms, chopped

½ sweet onion, chopped (see Appendix A, Tip #8)

4 ripe tomatoes, crushed

1 Tbsp. fresh oregano

2–4 Tbsp. fresh basil, chopped

½ cup scallions (green onions), chopped

½ cup cilantro

Veggie or sea salt and ground black pepper to taste

½ tsp. crushed red pepper flakes

Juice of 1 lemon

Directions

1. Wash all vegetables and shred the raw zucchini with a box grater.

2. Heat oil in a saucepan over high heat. Add garlic, mushrooms, and onion, and stir-fry until the garlic turns slightly golden.

3. Stir in tomatoes, oregano, basil, scallions, and cilantro. Reduce heat, cover, and simmer on reduced heat for 10–15 minutes.

4. Taste and add salt, pepper, and crushed red pepper flakes as needed. Add 1 tablespoon of lemon juice. Stir and simmer for another 10 minutes over low heat.

5. In a bowl, mix the zucchini, remaining lemon juice, salt, and pepper.

6. Serve the zucchini on plates topped with 2–3 tablespoons of the tomato sauce.

> **QUICK TIPS**
>
> - We often use organic maple syrup to sweeten sauces. After the Daniel fast you can add 1 teaspoon of organic maple syrup to this sauce.
> - We use the Cuisinart Vegetable Y Shredder, available from www.amazon.com.

Edamame Succotash *Serves 4*

2 cups fresh (or frozen) shelled edamame

2 cups calabaza squash, chopped into small cubes

4 Tbsp. olive oil

2–3 Tbsp. minced garlic

Veggie or sea salt and ground black pepper to taste

2–4 Tbsp. rice butter

Directions

1. Wash and rinse edamame and set aside.

2. Remove rind from squash (see Appendix A, Tip #1) and cut into cubes.

3. Heat olive oil in pan over high heat. Add garlic and sauté until golden brown.

4. Add chopped calabaza and sauté until fork-tender (see Appendix A, Tip #2).

5. Add edamame and mix all together. Simmer for 5–10 minutes.

6. Sprinkle with salt and pepper. Remove from stovetop, add butter, and serve.

Cumin and Lime Tofu *Serves 4*

2 Tbsp. minced garlic

½ tsp. cumin

Juice from ½ lime

Black pepper to taste

Veggie or sea salt to taste

¼ cup olive oil

2 cups firm tofu, cubed

6 romaine lettuce leaves, washed

Directions

1. In a deep bowl, stir together the garlic, cumin, lime juice, pepper, salt, and 2 tablespoons of olive oil.

2. Add tofu to the mixture, stirring until each piece is well coated. Cover and let marinate for 20 minutes.

3. In a pan over high heat, cook the tofu in remaining olive oil until very lightly browned.

4. Serve with 6 leaves of romaine lettuce and enjoy!

> ### AFTER-THE-FAST TIP
>
> During the fast this dish can be eaten with any vegetable dish whether steamed or stir-fried. We often eat this dish with any squash dish or any of the dishes already prepared.
>
> After the fast, our daughters love it with stir-fried rice noodles, over yellow rice, or over any rice dish with vegetables.

Yam and Squash Medley *Serves 4*

2 yams or sweet potatoes
1 yellow squash
1 zucchini squash
1 butternut squash
3 Tbsp. minced garlic
¼ cup olive oil

1 tsp. coriander
1 tsp. cinnamon
Veggie or sea salt and ground black
    pepper to taste
½ tsp. nutmeg
4 Tbsp. rice butter

Directions

1. Boil yams until fork-tender (see Appendix A, Tip #2). Drain, peel, and set aside.

2. While yams are boiling, wash and slice all three squashes.

3. In a wok or pan, sauté the garlic in olive oil, adding coriander and ½ tsp. of cinnamon. Add the squash and sauté until lightly browned. Season with salt and pepper to taste.

4. Cut the yams in half lengthwise and top with nutmeg and remaining cinnamon. Spread the rice butter on yams or sweet potatoes evenly.

5. Serve the squash along with the yams and a salad.

Spaghetti Squash Ceviche *Serves 4–6*

1 large spaghetti squash (or 2 medium-size squashes), halved

Juice of 6 lemons

Juice of 6 limes

2 Tbsp. ginger

3 Tbsp. minced garlic

2 jalapeño peppers, minced

4 scallions (green onions), thinly sliced

2 Tbsp. veggie or sea salt

2 Tbsp. black pepper

¼ cup olive oil

1 red bell pepper, finely diced

¼ cup cilantro, chopped

6 romaine lettuce leaves, washed

Directions

1. Cover squash with a wet paper towel and microwave on high until fork-tender (see Appendix A, Tip #2), approximately 5–6 minutes (microwave cooking times may vary).

2. Let cool slightly and remove the seeds from each half. Then use a fork to "rake" 4–6 cups of flesh out of the squash, creating strands that resemble spaghetti. Set aside.

3. In a large bowl combine the juices, ginger, garlic, peppers, scallions, salt, and pepper. Add the squash and mix. Cover and refrigerate for at least 2 hours.

4. Transfer the squash from the marinade to a serving bowl. Add olive oil, red pepper, and cilantro.

5. Serve on a bed of romaine lettuce.

Stuffed Sweet Potato Fritters *Serves 6*

3–4 sweet potatoes
½ cup olive oil
3 Tbsp. Ener-G Rice Flour
3 Tbsp. minced garlic
1 small green pepper, finely chopped
1 small red pepper, finely chopped

1 small red onion, finely chopped (see
Appendix A, Tip #8)
½ cup cilantro, finely chopped
1 lb. ground tofu
Veggie or sea salt and ground black
pepper to taste
2 tsp. Ener-G Egg Replacer

Directions

1. To a pot of *cold* salted water, add potatoes and bring to a boil. Cook until fork-tender (see Appendix A, Tip #2). Remove from stove, drain, and let cool.

2. In a skillet over high heat, combine olive oil, flour, garlic, peppers, onion, cilantro, and tofu. Mix well and sauté for 20 minutes. Add salt and pepper. Drain the liquid and set aside.

3. Peel the potatoes with a butter knife and add to a large bowl. Mash the sweet potatoes with a potato masher or handheld mixer until smooth. Add the Egg Replacer, following the instructions on the box for two eggs.

4. Take small portion of sweet potato mixture and roll it in the palm of your hands as though you were making a meatball.

5. On wax paper, flatten one sweet potato ball into a round. Spoon the pepper mixture in the center of the round and spread. Take another sweet potato ball, flatten it into a round, and use it to cover the pepper mixture like a sandwich. Use a fork to press the edges of the potato rounds together. Repeat until potato mixture is used up (about 6–8 fritters).

6. Spray a medium skillet with cooking spray. When heated, place 2–4 sweet potato fritters in the skillet. When brown on the first side, flip to allow the other side to brown. Remove from pan to a paper towel–lined plate to absorb excess oil before serving.

BAKING OPTION

If you prefer to bake your fritters instead of frying them, try the following:

- After completing step 3, combine the mixture from step 2 and the potatoes from step 3 together and mix well.
- Form into balls, place on a baking sheet, and flash freeze the potato balls (see Appendix A, Tip #12).
- Heat oven to 375 degrees, spray a baking sheet with cooking spray, and place the balls on the sheet. Bake uncovered for 20 minutes.

Lemon Pepper and Garlic Zucchini *Serves 4*

3 zucchini, cut into slices
1 Tbsp. minced garlic
2 Tbsp. lemon juice, squeezed
3–4 Tbsp. lemon pepper

Veggie or sea salt and ground black
  pepper to taste
¼ cup olive oil
½ cup fresh parsley, chopped

Directions

1. Preheat oven to 400 degrees.

2. After washing and slicing the zucchini, place zucchini slices in bowl.

3. Add garlic, lemon juice, lemon pepper, and salt and pepper to taste.

4. Pour the olive oil over the zucchini and mix all ingredients well.

5. Place on baking sheet and bake for approximately 15–20 minutes, or until fork-tender (see Appendix A, Tip #2).

6. Garnish with parsley and serve.

Broccoli Au Gratin *Serves 4*

2 heads broccoli or 2 10-oz. packages frozen broccoli florets
1 cup Vegenaise (mayo substitute)
1 cup rice mozzarella cheese
Veggie or sea salt and ground black pepper to taste
4 Tbsp. Ener-G Bread Crumbs

Directions

1. Preheat oven to 400 degrees.

2. Break the broccoli into florets and cook in lightly salted boiling water for 3–5 minutes or until fork-tender (see Appendix A, Tip #2). (If you are using frozen broccoli, bring light salted water to a boil, add florets, and boil for 5–7 minutes.) Drain and place in baking dish.

3. In a separate bowl, mix the Vegenaise, cheese, and salt and pepper to taste. Spoon over the broccoli florets.

4. Sprinkle Ener-G Bread Crumbs over the top of the dish. Place in oven and bake for 15–20 minutes or until golden brown.

Vegetables Au Gratin *Serves 4*

3 medium zucchini, sliced
2 cups cauliflower
1 cup Vegenaise (mayo substitute)
½ cup hemp milk
2 Tbsp. olive oil
¼ cup minced onions
2 Tbsp. minced garlic
½ tsp. dried dill

½ tsp. dried thyme
3 Tbsp. cilantro, chopped
1 cup rice mozzarella cheese
Veggie or sea salt and ground black
 pepper to taste
¼ cup rice Parmesan cheese
2 Tbsp. parsley, chopped

Directions

1. Preheat oven to 400 degrees.

2. Blanch zucchini in lightly salted boiling water for approximately 3–5 minutes. Remove, drain, and place in baking dish.

3. Repeat above step for cauliflower, letting it cook for approximately 5 minutes. Remove, drain, and place in the dish with the zucchini; mix together.

4. In a separate bowl, stir together the Vegenaise, milk, olive oil, onions, garlic, dill, thyme, cilantro, mozzarella cheese, and salt and pepper to taste.

5. Spoon the mixture over the vegetables and mix together.

6. Sprinkle with Parmesan cheese.

7. Bake in oven for 7–10 minutes or until golden brown.

8. Garnish with parsley, and serve.

Baked Fennel With Rice Mozzarella Cheese *Serves 4*

¼ cup olive oil
2–3 Tbsp. minced garlic
Veggie or sea salt to taste
2–3 lbs. fennel bulbs, washed

1½ cups shredded rice mozzarella cheese
½ cup rice Parmesan cheese

Directions

1. Preheat oven to 400 degrees.

2. In a pot, bring olive oil, garlic, and salt to a boil. Add fennel bulb and cook for approximately 3–5 minutes, or until fork-tender (see Appendix A, Tip #2). Drain well.

3. Cut fennel bulbs lengthways into 4 pieces. Place in baking dish and sprinkle with cheese.

4. Bake for approximately 15–20 minutes or until cheese is golden.

Zucchini With Sun-Dried Tomatoes *Serves 4*

10 sun-dried tomatoes packed in oil
¼ cup olive oil
1 onion, chopped
1 Tbsp. garlic

2 lbs. zucchini, cut into strips
Veggie or sea salt and ground black
pepper to taste
3 Tbsp. parsley, chopped

Directions

1. Slice the sun-dried tomatoes into thin strips. Place the tomatoes in a bowl with ¾ cup warm water. Let stand for approximately 15–20 minutes.

2. Heat olive oil in a large skillet. Add onion and cook until fork-tender (see Appendix A, Tip #2). Then add the garlic and the zucchini strips. Cook for approximately 5 minutes.

3. Add the tomatoes with water, and season with salt and pepper to taste. Mix all ingredients together and simmer, covered, for 5 minutes.

4. Remove from heat. Garnish with parsley and serve hot or cold. If serving cold, place dish into the refrigerator for 20 minutes and serve.

Ginger Stir-Fry *Serves 4–6*

3 Tbsp. tamari sauce
3 Tbsp. Bragg Liquid Aminos
4 Tbsp. minced garlic
2 Tbsp. lemon juice
2 Tbsp. lime juice
1 Tbsp. fresh ginger, peeled and grated
½ tsp. red pepper flakes
2 tsp. thyme
1 tsp. ground nutmeg
1 Tbsp. cilantro, chopped
Veggie or sea salt and ground black
    pepper to taste
1 package firm tofu, cut in 1-in. cubes
¼ cup water

¼ cup olive oil
1 cup broccoli florets
1 cup snow peas
1 cup baby bella mushrooms, sliced
½ cup water chestnuts (no sodium
    added), drained
3 stalks celery, chopped
2 sweet onions, cut diagonally (see
    Appendix A, Tip #8)
½ cup bamboo shoots (no sodium
    added), drained
2 Tbsp. parsley, chopped

Directions

1. In a bowl, mix tamari sauce, Bragg Liquid Aminos, 3 tablespoons garlic, lemon juice, lime juice, ginger, red pepper flakes, thyme, ground nutmeg, cilantro, and salt and pepper to taste.

2. Add the tofu to mixture, and let it sit for at least 20 minutes.

3. Heat large, nonstick skillet over high heat and add water, olive oil, 1 tablespoon garlic, and salt; bring to boil.

4. Add broccoli florets. Cook for 1 minute and remove.

5. Add snow peas, mushrooms, water chestnuts, and celery to the boiling water. Cook for 2 minutes, then remove and drain excess water.

6. Combine the broccoli florets with the remaining vegetables and stir in the mixture with the tofu. Mix well.

7. Add the bamboo shoots, and cook until tender-crisp.

8. Garnish with parsley before serving.

Italian Sautéed Beans   *Serves 4*

¼ cup olive oil
3 Tbsp. minced garlic
1 bag fresh baby spinach leaves
1 cup fresh baby bellamushrooms, sliced
2 tomatoes, diced
½ cup roasted red peppers, diced
2 15-oz. cans cannellini beans
¼ cup Bragg Liquid Aminos

1 tsp. dried Italian seasoning
½ cup fresh cilantro
Veggie or sea salt and ground black
   pepper to taste
¼ cup fresh basil, chopped
1 cup rice mozzarella cheese

Directions

1. In a large skillet, heat olive oil over high heat.

2. Add garlic, spinach leaves, mushrooms, tomatoes, roasted peppers, beans, Bragg Liquid Aminos, Italian seasoning, cilantro, and salt and pepper to taste. Stir and cook for approximately 5–10 minutes, or until the beans are fork-tender (see Appendix A, Tip #2).

3. Add basil and reduce heat to low. Cook for approximately for 2–3 minutes.

4. Garnish with rice mozzarella cheese. Let stand for 2–3 minutes or until the cheese melts, then serve.

Stir-Fried Asparagus   *Serves 4*

1½ lbs. asparagus
¼ cup olive oil
1 Tbsp. minced garlic
Veggie or sea salt and ground black pepper to taste

Directions

1. Wash asparagus and trim ends, then cut diagonally in 3-inch pieces.

2. In a large skillet, heat olive oil over high heat. Add the garlic. Stir until garlic is slightly golden.

3. Add the asparagus to the skillet and cook for 3 minutes, constantly stirring. Promptly remove.

4. Add salt and pepper to taste, then serve.

Sautéed Cucumbers *Serves 4*

3 medium cucumbers
¼ cup olive oil
1 tsp. minced garlic
½ red bell pepper, diced

Veggie or sea salt and ground black
   pepper to taste
1 tsp. lemon juice

Directions

1. Cut each cucumber in 1-inch slices crosswise.

2. In a skillet over medium heat, add olive oil and garlic.

> **QUICK TIP**
>
> If the cucumbers are not organic, then remove the skin or wash with veggie wash.

3. Add bell pepper, cucumbers, and salt and pepper to taste. Cook for approximately 7–10 minutes.

4. Remove from heat add lemon juice. Mix well and serve.

Asparagus With Sliced Almonds and Creamy Lemon Sauce *Serves 4*

2 Tbsp. freshly squeezed lemon juice
½ cup Vegenaise (mayo substitute)
1 Tbsp. minced garlic
1 tsp. chives
Veggie or sea salt and ground black
   pepper to taste

¼ cup olive oil
¼ cup sliced almonds
2 lbs. fresh asparagus, cut diagonally in
   3-in. pieces

Directions

1. In a bowl, add lemon juice, Vegenaise, garlic, chives, and salt and pepper to taste. Mix well.

2. In a skillet, heat olive oil over medium heat. Add the almonds and cook until lightly brown.

3. Add the asparagus and mix well. Add salt and pepper to taste. Cover for approximately 3–7 minutes.

4. Remove from heat and pour lemon mixture over the asparagus and serve.

Chapter 3

RAW SIDES AND SALADS

...the Lord stood at his side.
—ACTS 23:11

Apple-Cranberry-Mandarin Spinach Salad *Serves 4*

1 bunch fresh spinach
¼ cup dried cranberries
1 apple (any variety), cored and sliced diagonally
¼ cup walnuts, chopped
2 mandarin oranges, divided into segments or 1 naval orange, segmented

Directions

1. Wash the spinach in a large bowl of cold water.

2. Dry spinach in a salad spinner (see Appendix A, Tip #5).

3. After the spinach is dry, give it a coarse chop and place in a large salad bowl.

4. Add cranberries, apple, walnuts, and mandarin orange.

5. Mix all together and serve with one of the salad dressings in chapter 5.

Raw Vegetable Platter *Serves 6–8*

2–3 Tbsp. minced garlic
4–5 asparagus spears
½ cup broccoli
1 zucchini, diced
¼ cup olive oil
Juice of 1 lemon
Veggie or sea salt and ground black
   pepper to taste
1 red onion, sliced diagonally (see
   Appendix A, Tip #8)

2 ripe tomatoes, sliced diagonally
4–6 artichoke hearts
½ cup carrots, shredded
2 cups bok choy, thinly sliced (use the
   white portion of this vegetable)
1 yellow squash, sliced diagonally
½ cup beets, shredded
½ cup Jerusalem artichoke
½ cup jícama
4–6 romaine lettuce leaves (whole)

Directions

1. In a 1-quart pan bring 2–4 cups salted water to a boil, adding 1 tablespoon of garlic.

2. Dip the asparagus into the boiling water for 5 seconds; remove promptly and set aside.

3. Dip broccoli in boiling water for the same time and set aside to cool.

4. In a small bowl combine the zucchini, olive oil, lemon juice, and remaining garlic. Season with salt and pepper and place the bowl in the center of a serving platter.

5. Add remaining ingredients around the platter and enjoy.

6. Serve with your choice of salad dressing (chapter 5), guacamole (chapter 3), or hummus (chapter 3).

What Is Jícama?

Jícama (pronounced HIH-kuh-ma) is a root vegetable that can be found at farmer's markets, ethnic markets that feature Hispanic foods, and sometimes at your local grocery store. It's brown and husky on the outside and must be peeled before eating. The white, juicy inside has a mild, nondescript flavor but a nice crunchy texture.

Spinach and Jerusalem Artichoke Salad *Serves 4*

2 cups organic fresh spinach
Juice of 1 lemon
4 Tbsp. olive oil
1 Tbsp. minced garlic
1 cup Jerusalem artichoke, sliced

4 Tbsp. black olives, chopped
4 Tbsp. green olives, chopped
2 Tbsp. dried cranberry
Veggie or sea salt and ground black
  pepper to taste

Directions

1. Wash the spinach in a large bowl of cold water.

2. Dry spinach in a salad spinner (see Appendix A, Tip #5).

3. After the spinach is dry, give it a coarse chop and place in a large salad bowl.

4. Add remaining ingredients to bowl, toss, and serve with one of the salad dressings from chapter 5.

QUICK SUBSTITUTIONS FOR JERUSALEM ARTICHOKES

- If Jerusalem artichoke is out of season or you are pressed for time, you can substitute frozen artichoke hearts, such as the ones available from Birdseye. Artichoke hearts are less crunchy, but their flavor is similar to that of Jerusalem artichokes. We recommend frozen artichoke hearts over jarred or canned because the frozen variety tastes fresher and does not have the briny flavor of its jarred or canned counterparts.
- You can also try water chestnuts or jícama as a substitute. They have similar texture to Jerusalem artichokes but a completely different flavor.

Zucchini Salad With Lemon, Lime, and Cilantro *Serves 4*

3–4 zucchini, cubed
¼ cup olive oil
3–4 Tbsp. minced garlic
Juice of 1 lemon

Juice of 1 lime
½ cup cilantro
Veggie or sea salt and ground black
pepper to taste

Directions

1. In a large salad bowl, combine zucchini, olive oil, garlic, 1 tablespoon each of lemon and lime juice, cilantro, salt, and pepper. Mix until zucchini is evenly coated with other ingredients. Leave a tablespoon of cilantro for garnishing.

2. Cover and refrigerate for approximately 10–15 minutes, or you can leave refrigerated overnight.

3. Garnish with the cilantro and serve with a garden salad.

> **TRY IT GRILLED OR RAW!**
>
> For this recipe you can use either grilled or raw zucchini. For grilling, the preparation of the zucchini is the same. Coat the zucchini with the mixture before grilling, and allow it to marinate for approximately 10–15 minutes. If you have a temperature gauge on your grill, heat it up to 400 degrees and grill for approximately 3–5 minutes. You can serve this dish warm right from the grill or refrigerate for 10–15 minutes, garnish, and serve cold with a salad.

Daniel's Carrot Salad *Serves 4–6*

2–3 Tbsp. Vegenaise (mayo substitute)
4 Tbsp. minced garlic
1 tsp. veggie or sea salt
½ tsp. chili powder
Juice from half a lemon
1 tsp. fresh dill, chopped

6–7 carrots, shredded
2 Tbsp. dried cranberries
1 green apple, cored and chopped
¼ cup cilantro, chopped
2–3 Tbsp. fresh parsley, chopped

Directions

1. In a bowl, combine first six ingredients. Mix well, then add carrots, cranberries, and apple. Toss until evenly coated.

2. Cover and refrigerate for 2 hours. Just before serving, sprinkle with cilantro and parsley as a garnish.

> **TIME-SAVING TIP**
>
> Buy a bag of organic shredded carrots if you don't have time to peel and shred them yourself.

Avocado and Gala Apple Salad *Serves 4*

½ cup golden raisins
2 ripe Hass avocados
1 Gala apple
2 Tbsp. olive oil

Juice of ½ lemon
20 pimento-stuffed olives
2 Tbsp. fresh mint, chopped
2 Tbsp. cilantro, chopped

Directions

1. Soak the raisins in warm water for 10–15 minutes to plump them up.

2. While raisins are soaking, cut each avocado in half and slice into thin lengthwise slices (see Appendix A, Tip #6).

3. Slice the apple lengthwise.

4. Arrange the avocado and apple slices on a plate. Gently drizzle with olive oil and lemon juice.

5. Drain raisins and pat dry. Add raisins and olives to the plate.

6. Garnish with mint and cilantro and serve.

Avocado and Kale Salad *Serves 4–6*

1 bundle of kale
1 small red onion, thinly sliced (see Appendix A, Tip #8)
2 Hass avocados, cubed (see Appendix A, Tip #6)
¼ cup scallions (green onions), sliced
¼ cup cilantro, chopped

Directions

1. Soak kale in cold water and wash leaves individually.
2. Place kale leaves on cutting board, cut thinly, and place in salad spinner (see Appendix A, Tip #5) to remove all excess water. Transfer kale from spinner to a large bowl.
3. Place red onion slices in bowl.
4. Place avocado cubes in bowl.
5. Toss the scallions and cilantro in bowl.
6. Toss and serve with a salad dressing from chapter 5.

QUICK TIPS

As an alternative to kale you can use rainbow chard or the green leaves of bok choy. Bok choy, a member of the cabbage family, has thick white stalk and dark green leaves. It has a sweet flavor and crisp texture and is high in vitamins A and C, high in calcium, and low in calories.

Kale belongs to the brassica family, which includes brussels sprouts and collards. It is a low-glycemic food, so it aids in weight loss. Kale has been shown to have anticancer benefits because of its sulfur-containing phytonutrients. It's also a great source of calcium. For further information, see www.whole-food-supplements-guide.com/what-is-kale.html.

Cucumber and Sweet Onion Salad *Serves 4–6*

2 cucumbers, thinly sliced

1 large sweet onion, thinly sliced (see Appendix A, Tip #8)

3–4 Tbsp. cilantro, chopped

4 Tbsp. garlic

3–5 Tbsp. scallions (green onions), chopped

Juice of 2 lemons

Veggie or sea salt and ground black pepper to taste

Louisiana Hot Sauce (optional)

¼ cup olive oil

Directions

1. Place cucumber and onion slices in large bowl. Add cilantro, garlic, and scallions to the mixture.

2. Pour lemon juice over the entire mixture and sprinkle with salt and pepper to taste.

3. Add Louisiana Hot Sauce to taste, if desired.

4. Toss with olive oil and mix until all ingredients are evenly coated. Add more seasoning if needed, and serve.

QUICK TIPS

- Peel the cucumber skin off if it is not organic or if the cucumber is waxy.
- You can scrape the cucumber skin lengthwise with a fork so it has a ridged pattern when sliced. For a twist, add cherry tomatoes to this salad; just cut them into halves before tossing with the cucumber onion mixture.
- This is a great salad to make ahead of time. Simply cover and place in refrigerator until ready to serve. This salad can last up to a week in the fridge.

Zucchini and Carrot Salad *Serves 4*

4 zucchini, shredded
1 medium/large carrot, shredded
Juice of 1 large lemon (or 2 small lemons)
2 Tbsp. Vegenaise (mayo substitute) (or
   2–3 Tbsp. olive oil)
4 Tbsp. minced garlic

Veggie or sea salt and ground black
   pepper to taste

Directions

1. Place the shredded zucchini and carrot in a bowl.

2. Add the lemon juice, Vegenaise or olive oil, garlic, pepper, and salt, and mix well.

3. Add more seasoning, if needed, before serving.

QUICK TIP

We use Vegenaise when we want a creamier salad, and we refrigerate it if it is not going to be eaten right away. Otherwise, we enjoy it with the olive oil or use one of the salad dressings from chapter 5.

Raw Vegetable Medley Salad *Serves 6–8*

1 head cauliflower
1 head broccoli
½ head cabbage, shredded
½ cup olive oil

2 Tbsp. minced garlic
Veggie or sea salt and ground black
   pepper to taste
Juice of 2 lemons

Directions

1. Wash and section the cauliflower and broccoli into florets and place in bowl. Add the cabbage and mix well.

2. In a separate bowl whisk the olive oil, garlic, salt, pepper, and lemon juice, and then pour over the vegetables.

3. Mix and let sit, covered, for 10–15 minutes before serving.

QUICK TIP

You can also eat this salad with the hummus or guacamole dips. Eating the vegetables raw increases your fiber intake, and it's very chewy. I enjoy raw food because it fills you quicker and seems to keep you full longer.

Vegetable Fest *Serves 4*

½ cup broccoli florets
½ cup sweet onion, cut diagonally (see
    Appendix A, Tip #8)
½ cup red onion, cut diagonally
½ cup carrots, shredded (or 1 cup carrots,
    cut diagonally)
2 stalks baby bok choy, cut thinly
1 red pepper, deveined and sliced
    lengthwise

1 yellow pepper, deveined and sliced
    lengthwise
½ cup olive oil
3 Tbsp. minced garlic
Juice of 1 lemon
½ cup scallions (green onions)
1 tsp. chives
Veggie or sea salt and ground black
    pepper to taste

Directions

1. Wash all vegetables.

2. Toss broccoli, onions, and carrots into a salad spinner (see Appendix A, Tip #5) to remove any excess water, and then place them in a large bowl.

3. Toss cut bok choy into salad spinner, then add to veggies in the large bowl.

4. Spin the peppers in the salad spinner, then toss into the bowl.

5. In a separate bowl whisk olive oil, garlic, lemon juice, scallions, chives, salt, and pepper. Pour over the ingredients in large bowl and mix well.

6. Cover, and let sit for 20 minutes before serving.

ALTERNATIVES TO SERVING RAW VEGGIES

Some people find it challenging to eat this much raw food. Another way to eat these vegetables is as follows. In a large pot, boil 4 cups salted water, adding ¼ cup olive oil and 3 tablespoons of garlic. Place vegetables in boiling water for 20–30 seconds, drain, and transfer to a bowl. Follow the directions above. This makes the vegetables tender and easier to chew. (You can do this for most raw food.) You can also use the dips in chapter 3.

Zucchini and Squash Medley Salad *Serves 4–6*

2–4 zucchini, cut into long strips
2–4 yellow squashes, cut into long strips
¼ cup olive oil
2 Tbsp. minced garlic
½ cup cilantro

2–4 Tbsp. lemon juice
Veggie or sea salt and ground black pepper to taste

Directions

1. Place zucchini and squash strips in a bowl.

2. In a separate bowl, whisk olive oil, garlic, cilantro, lemon juice, salt, and pepper. Pour over the zucchini and squash.

3. Mix all ingredients well and let sit, covered, for 30 minutes before serving.

ALTERNATIVE IDEAS

This dish can be served raw or cooked. If cooked, it can be served over brown rice, a bed of wheat- and gluten-free pasta (i.e., penne pasta), or rice pasta (after you finish the fast).

If you decide to cook this dish, here are two cooking options:

1. Boil 4 cups salted water, adding 2 tablespoons of olive oil and 1 tablespoon of garlic. Place the zucchini and squash in boiling water for 2–5 minutes, then promptly remove and place in bowl. Cover the vegetables with the mixture from step 2 above, mix well, and serve.

2. Sauté the garlic in olive oil in a pan. Add the zucchini and squash and sauté until golden brown. Add cilantro, lemon juice, salt, and pepper. Promptly remove from heat when vegetables are tender.

Jícama, Cucumber, and Avocado Salad *Serves 4*

½ jícama, diced
1–2 cucumbers, diced
  (see Appendix A, Tip #10)
Juice of 1 lemon
Juice of 1 lime
½ cup cilantro
2–3 Tbsp. minced garlic
½ cup olive oil
1 small sweet onion, cut diagonally (see
  Appendix A, Tip #8)

½ cup red onion, diced
½ tsp. crushed red pepper
Veggie or sea salt and ground black
  pepper to taste
1–2 avocados, diced in large pieces (see
  Appendix A, Tip #6)
1 head romaine lettuce, chopped

Directions

1. Mix the jícama, cucumbers, lemon juice, lime juice, cilantro, garlic, olive oil, onions, and red pepper in a large bowl.

2. Add salt and pepper to taste. Depending on your taste, you may add more lemon or lime juice.

3. Gently fold avocado into the ingredients. (Don't stir too much or the avocado will start to mash up.) Add more pepper if needed.

4. Cover tightly and refrigerate for 30 minutes, then serve over a bed of romaine lettuce.

Kale and Bok Choy Salad *Serves 4–6*

4–6 stalks kale (rainbow, red, or green),
    coarsely chopped
3–4 stalks bok choy, coarsely chopped
4 large radishes, sliced
1 cucumber, sliced
2 stalks scallions (green onions),
    cut into 2-inch pieces
2 tomatoes, seeded and diced
    (see Appendix A, Tip #7)
½ red onion, cut diagonally
    (see Appendix A, Tip #8)
6–10 green olives, halved
6–10 black olives, halved
4 Tbsp. lemon juice
¼ cup olive oil
4 Tbsp. minced garlic
1 Tbsp. fresh dill
Veggie or sea salt and ground
    black pepper to taste

TIME-SAVING TIP

Chop, dice, and slice your veggies (radishes, cucumbers, scallions, tomatoes, onions, and olives) ahead of time and store them in tightly sealed containers in the refrigerator for 24–48 hours before adding them to the salad greens.

Directions

1. Mix first nine ingredients in a large salad bowl.

2. In a separate bowl whisk lemon juice, olive oil, garlic, dill, salt, and pepper. Use this mixture as a salad dressing.

Stuffed Endive Wraps *Serves 4–6*

1 head of Belgian endive

1 plum tomato, seeded and diced
  (see Appendix A, Tip #7)

1 Hass avocado, cubed (see Appendix A,
  Tip #6)

1 Tbsp. minced garlic

1 shallot, thinly sliced

¼ cup olive oil

Veggie or sea salt and ground black
  pepper to taste

Directions

1. Separate the endive leaves and wash. Put in salad spinner (see Appendix A, Tip #5) to remove excess water.

2. Put tomato and avocado in a bowl. Set aside.

3. In a pan over high heat, sauté the garlic and shallot in olive oil, seasoning with salt and pepper. Remove from heat and let cool for 7–10 minutes.

4. Pour the garlic and shallot mixture over the tomato and avocado, and mix well.

5. Spoon tomato mixture into the middle of each endive leaf, and wrap or fold the leaf around the mixture.

6. Chill in refrigerator for approximately 10 minutes before serving.

QUICK FACTS ABOUT BELGIAN ENDIVE

- Belgian endive has a small head of long, cream-colored leaves. It is cultivated entirely in the dark to keep the leaves from turning green.
- Don't confuse it with escarole or curly endive, which are broader, larger, green-leafed vegetables.
- Belgian endive is also called Belgian chicory, Brussels chicory, blanching chicory, chicon, Dutch chicory, French endive, *witloof* (Flemish for "white leaf"), or witloof chicory.
- You can substitute Belgian endive with radicchio, arugula, or watercress.

Jícama, Avocado, and Edamame Salad *Serves 4*

1 jícama, peeled and cubed
2 Hass avocados, cubed (see Appendix
   A, Tip #6)
1 cup shelled edamame
1 English cucumber or regular cucumber,
   cubed
   (see Appendix A, Tip #10)

1 Tbsp. minced garlic
2 Tbsp. olive oil
½ cup cilantro, finely chopped
Juice of 1 lime
Veggie or sea salt and ground black
   pepper to taste

Directions

1. Place jícama, avocado, edamame, and cucumber in a large bowl.

2. In a separate bowl, combine garlic, olive oil, cilantro, lime juice, salt, and pepper.

3. Pour lime mixture over vegetables. Mix well, then chill approximately 10–15 minutes before serving.

Crunchy Raw Salad *Serves 4*

½ jícama, thinly sliced
1 large white turnip, chopped
1 cup Jerusalem artichoke, sliced
Juice of 1 lime
1 Tbsp. minced garlic
½ sweet onion, chopped (see Appendix
   A, Tip #8)

½ cup cilantro, chopped
½ cup scallions (green onions)
1 Tbsp. fresh dill
½ cup olive oil
Veggie or sea salt and ground black
   pepper to taste

Directions

1. Mix the jícama, turnip, and artichoke in a bowl.

2. In a separate bowl combine the lime juice, garlic, onion, cilantro, scallions, dill, olive oil, salt, and pepper.

3. Pour lime mixture over the salad and refrigerate for 20 minutes before serving.

Daniel Fast Green Salad *Serves 4*

2 cups spinach

2 cups romaine lettuce

1 cup watercress

½ cup red bell pepper, diced

2 tomatoes, seeded and diced (see Appendix A, Tip #7)

1 cup carrots, grated

½ cup celery, chopped

½ cup cilantro

½ cup scallions (green onions), chopped

½ cup dried cranberries

2 avocados, peeled and cubed (see Appendix A, Tip #6)

Directions

1. Wash all vegetables. Then put all leafy vegetables into a salad spinner (see Appendix A, Tip #5). When they are sufficiently dried, transfer them to a large bowl.

2. Add remaining ingredients to the bowl.

3. Toss and serve.

> ### SALAD DRESSING SUGGESTION
>
> We recommend serving this salad with one of the salad dressings in chapter 5.

Daniel Fast Emerald Salad *Serves 4*

2–3 large tomatoes, seeded and diced (see Appendix A, Tip #7)

2 cucumbers, seeded and diced (see Appendix A, Tip #10)

1 green bell pepper, seeded and diced

1 large red onion, diced (see Appendix A, Tip #8)

1 cup scallions (green onions), thinly sliced

1 cup cilantro, chopped

Directions

1. Combine all ingredients in a large salad bowl, toss, and serve.

> ### SALAD DRESSING SUGGESTION
>
> We recommend serving this salad with Tahini Salad Dressing (chapter 5).

Hummus With Cilantro and Scallions *Serves 6–8*

1 15-oz. can organic garbanzo beans (chickpeas), drained and rinsed
5 Tbsp. garlic
¼ cup tahini
½ cup olive oil
Juice of 2 lemons

¼ cup cilantro
¼ cup scallions (green onions)
1 large carrot
4 celery stalks
Veggie or sea salt and ground black pepper to taste

Directions

1. Place the following ingredients in a food processor: garbanzo beans, garlic, tahini, olive oil, and the juice of 1 lemon. Begin processing (or blend on the "chop" setting if your food processor has one), checking constantly until all ingredients are chopped.

2. Add remaining ingredients and process until well blended. Sprinkle with salt and pepper. Process again to make sure all ingredients are well blended. Consistency should be similar to that of a sour cream–based dip for veggies or chips.

3. Add more salt and pepper if needed. Serve with raw vegetables. You can stuff hummus into celery stalks or use it as dip for carrots, peppers, cucumbers, etc.

Quick Tips

- We have a small food chopper that we attach to our blender. If your blender came with this type of attachment, this is the perfect recipe to use it!
- For creamier, lighter hummus, add 1 tablespoon of the grape seed variety of Vegenaise (mayo substitute).

Cilantro Dip *Serves 6–8*

1 cup Vegenaise (mayo substitute)
½ cup chopped cilantro
¼ cup scallions (green onions), thinly
   sliced

1 Tbsp lemon juice
1 Tbsp. minced garlic
Veggie or sea salt and ground black
   pepper to taste

Directions

1. In a bowl stir together in all ingredients, adding salt and pepper to taste.

2. Cover and chill for at least 4 hours. Serve with raw vegetables

Curry Dip *Serves 4–6*

1 cup Vegenaise (mayo substitute)
1 Tbsp. chili powder
1 Tbsp. lemon juice
1 Tbsp. minced garlic

½ tsp. curry powder
1 Tbsp. grated onion
Veggie or sea salt and ground black
   pepper to taste

Directions

1. In a bowl stir together in all ingredients, adding salt and pepper to taste.

2. Cover and chill for at least 4 hours. Serve with raw vegetables.

Papaya Salad *Serves 6–10*

1 green papaya, peeled and shredded
   (see Appendix A, Tip #9)
1 cup carrots, shredded
1 zucchini, diced
½ red bell pepper, seeded and diced
1 green chili pepper, thinly sliced

½ cup scallions (green onions), thinly
   sliced
2 Tbsp. lemon juice
1 Tbsp. mint leaves
¼ cup olive oil
Veggie or sea salt and ground black
   pepper to taste

Directions

1. Combine all ingredients in a bowl. Mix well, season with salt and pepper, and serve.

"IF YOU CAN'T TAKE THE HEAT..."

If you can't take the heat of chili peppers—or hotter varieties—carefully remove all seeds and membranes before dicing. The seeds and membranes are the parts of the pepper that really pack the heat!

Daniel's Haroset (traditional Passover Seder dish)

Serves 4–6

2 Granny Smith apples, finely chopped
¾ cup golden raisins
1 cup pitted dates, chopped
¾ cup walnuts, finely chopped
¾ cup blanched almonds, finely chopped
1 tsp. ground cinnamon
½ tsp. ground ginger

½ tsp. black pepper
½ tsp. cloves
3 Tbsp. pomegranate juice
3 Tbsp. orange juice
2–3 Tbsp. kosher 100% Concord grape juice
1 tsp. orange zest

Directions

1. Mix the fruit, nuts, and spices in a serving bowl.
2. Stir in the three juices and orange zest. You may add more grape juice, if needed, before serving.

AFTER-THE-FAST TIP

After your fast, if preferred, you can swap out 2–3 tablespoons of kosher sweet red wine in place of the grape juice.

WHAT IS HAROSET?

Haroset, also known as *Charoset*, is a sweet dark colored chunky paste made of fruits and nuts serve primarily during the Passover Seder. Its color and texture are meant to recall the mortar with which the Israelites bonded bricks when they were enslaved in ancient Egypt. The word *Haroset* comes from the Hebrew word *cheres*, meaning "clay." For further information, see www.jewishrecipes.org/jewish-foods/charoset.html.

WHAT IS PASSOVER SEDER?

The Passover Seder is a ritual banquet that reenacts the Exodus of the Israelites from their time of slavery in ancient Egypt. The significant aspect of the Seder is the reading of the Haggadah, which relates in detail the events of the Exodus. The Seder is a customary occasion for Jewish families to gather together to reinforce their ties to Judaism. For further information, see http://www.ou.org/chagim/pesach/pesachguide/maze/basic5.htm.

Note: To make this dish authentic for Passover, all ingredients should be kosher!

Spicy Carrots Tzimmes (traditional Rosh Hashanah dish)

Serves 4

2 cups organic carrots, sliced
¼ cup olive oil
2 Tbsp. minced garlic
1 tsp. cumin
1 red chili pepper, seeded and chopped
Juice of 1 lemon
2 Tbsp. maple syrup

1 tsp. cinnamon
1 Tbsp. fresh mint
¼ cup cilantro
¼ cup scallions (green onions), thinly sliced
Veggie or sea salt to taste

Directions

1. Place carrots in 2–4 cups cold, salted water and bring to a boil. Boil until fork-tender. (Be careful not to overcook; they should be firm but tender.) Drain and set aside.

2. In a saucepan over high heat, heat oil. Add garlic, cumin, chili pepper, and lemon juice.

3. Add carrots and maple syrup to saucepan and sprinkle with cinnamon, stirring constantly until the liquid evaporates.

4. Remove from heat, and carefully place into serving dish. Sprinkle with mint, cilantro, scallions, and salt.

WHAT IS ROSH HASHANAH?

Rosh Hashanah is a Jewish holiday commonly referred to as the Jewish New Year. It is the first of the high holidays; specifically, it is set aside to focus on repentance, which concludes with the holiday of Yom Kippur. For further information, see www.jewfaq .org/holiday2.htm.

WHAT DOES *KOSHER* MEAN?

To make this dish authentic for Rosh Hashannah, all ingredients should be kosher. Kosher food is food that meets Jewish dietary laws. These foods must be prepared in accordance with *Kashrut*, which is the Hebrew word for "fit or proper." For further information, see www.jewfaq.org/kashrut.htm.

WHAT IS TZIMMES?

Tzimmes is traditionally served during Rosh Hashannah. The carrots symbolize the hope to increase good deeds in the coming year and are symbolic of gold coins, while the maple syrup symbolizes the hope that the next year will be sweeter. For further information, see www.koshercooking.com/recipes/passover/carrotzi.html.

Daniel's Authentic Guacamole *Serves 4–6*

4 Hass avocados, peeled (see Appendix
  A, Tip #6)
1 Tbsp. veggie or sea salt
1 Tbsp. Vegenaise (mayo substitute)
½ vine-ripe tomato, finely chopped

½ sweet onion, finely chopped (see
  Appendix A, Tip #8)
1 Serrano pepper, finely minced
2 Tbsp. water
Juice of ½ lemon
Juice of ½ lime

Directions

1. When peeling avocados, reserve one of the stones (seeds) for use in step 4.

2. Blend avocados in a food processor or blender until smooth.

3. Add remaining ingredients to food processor, saving the lemon and lime juice to add last. Add the juice as the processor is blending the other ingredients.

4. Spoon your guacamole into a serving bowl, and put one of the stones (seed) into the bowl. (Placing the avocado stone in the mixture will prevent it from turning brown.) Cover and refrigerate for about an hour.

5. Serve with chips, veggies, or along with a salad.

> ### WHY DO WE SPECIFY USING HASS AVOCADOS?
>
> Only use Hass avocados, which are small and brownish black in appearance. Do not use the large green avocados for this recipe. Hass avocados are traditionally used to make guacamole because the fruit is rich and creamy and is best suited to this traditional native Mexican dish.

> ### HAND-MASHING OPTION
>
> Some people prefer to mash avocados with a fork or potato masher for a chunkier texture. If you choose this option, simply combine the ingredients in a bowl and use a fork to mash the ingredients together.

Bean Salad *Serves 4*

1 package frozen Italian green beans (or fresh), cooked and drained

1 15-oz. can garbanzo beans (chickpeas), drained

1 cup celery, sliced

1 small red onion, thinly sliced (see Appendix A, Tip #8)

Salad dressing of your choice (see chapter 5)

1 head romaine or Boston lettuce

Directions

1. Toss all ingredients except lettuce in a salad bowl until well coated with salad dressing. Cover and chill overnight.

2. Serve on romaine or Boston lettuce.

Edamame and Black Olive Salad *Serves 4*

1 lb. shelled edamame, frozen or fresh

2 cups black pitted olives

½ cup green olives

1 red and 1 yellow pepper, cut diagonally

1 red onion, cut diagonally (see Appendix A, Tip #8)

½ cup sliced white mushrooms

½ cup cilantro

Juice of 1 lemon

1 tsp. chives

¼ cup olive oil

Veggie or sea salt and ground black pepper to taste

4 cups romaine lettuce or field greens (spring mix)

Directions

1. Thaw the edamame if using frozen. Put thawed or fresh edamame in a colander to drain. Transfer to a large bowl.

2. In the same bowl, add the olives, peppers, onion, mushrooms, cilantro, lemon juice, chives, and olive oil. Mix well and add salt and pepper to taste.

3. Chill for approximately 1 hour.

4. Serve over romaine lettuce or field greens.

Quinoa-Pecan Salad With Raisins and Cranberries

Serves 4

1½ cups quinoa
½ cup dried cranberries, soaked and drained
¼ cup golden raisins, soaked and drained
¾ cup pecans, finely chopped
½ cup cilantro, finely chopped

½ cup scallions (green onions), finely chopped
1 cup celery, finely diced
3–4 Tbsp. lemon juice
¼ cup olive oil
½ tsp. sesame oil
Veggie or sea salt and ground black pepper to taste

Directions

1. Boil 2–4 cups salted water in a medium-size pot. Add quinoa, stir, cover, and reduce heat. Simmer until the quinoa is soft, then remove from heat uncovered.

2. In a bowl combine cranberries, raisins, pecans, cilantro, scallions, celery, lemon juice, olive oil, sesame oil, salt, and pepper.

3. Add the quinoa to the bowl and mix thoroughly.

4. Cover dish with plastic wrap and let sit for 10 minutes before serving.

WHAT IS QUINOA?

Quinoa (pronounced "kin-wa") is a grain-like crop that has become highly appreciated for its nutritional value. It is an excellent source of protein and fiber as well as phosphorous, magnesium, and iron. It can be prepared as a hot breakfast cereal or substituted in recipes that would traditionally use rice.

Quinoa also makes a healthy alternative for wheat pasta because it is gluten-free and easy to digest. Companies such as Ancient Harvest offer quinoa in traditional pasta shapes such as spaghetti, elbow macaroni, and shells. For more information, visit www.quinoa.net.

Blanched Mixed Vegetable Salad *Serves 4*

¼ cup olive oil

3 Tbsp. minced garlic

¼ tsp. lemon juice

1 tsp. crushed red pepper

2 bay leaves

2 sprigs thyme

2 Tbsp. parsley

¼ cup tamari

¼ cup Bragg Liquid Aminos

½ cup sesame tahini (stir well before using)

2 cups cauliflower florets

1 red, 1 yellow, and 1 green pepper, diced

2 cups red cabbage, shredded

2 zucchini, diced

2 cups celery, diced

1 sweet onion, diced (see Appendix A, Tip #8)

1 red onion, diced

2 cups mushrooms, halved

3 tomatoes, diced (see Appendix A, Tip #7)

1 cup fennel, sliced

Veggie or sea salt and ground black pepper to taste

½ cup cilantro

Directions

1. In a small bowl, combine olive oil, garlic, lemon juice, crushed red pepper, bay leaves, thyme, parsley, tamari, Bragg Liquid Aminos, and tahini. Whisk together. Let sit, covered, for 30 minutes at room temperature.

2. Meanwhile, in a pot, boil 4 cups of salted water, adding a tablespoon of garlic and 2 tablespoons of olive oil. When the water comes to a boil, add cauliflower florets and boil for approximately 30 seconds and remove promptly. Place cauliflower florets in large bowl.

3. Repeat step 2 three more times for the peppers, red cabbage, and zucchini, adding veggies to the cauliflower in the large bowl each time. Refrigerate for 10 minutes.

4. Remove the vegetable bowl from the refrigerator and add the remaining vegetables. Mix well, adding salt and pepper to taste.

5. Pour the marinade sauce from step 1 over the vegetables and toss until evenly coated.

6. Garnish with cilantro and serve.

OPTION

Serve this salad over a bed of romaine lettuce if more greens are desired.

Tofu and Mixed Vegetable Salad *Serves 4*

½ cup olive oil
2 Tbsp. minced garlic
2 Tbsp. tamari
¼ cup lemon juice
Veggie or sea salt and ground black
   pepper to taste
1 pack of firm tofu, diced

4 cups broccoli florets
3 cups cherry tomatoes, halved
¼ cup black or kalamata olives, sliced
1 cup celery, diced
1 cup carrots, sliced
¼ sliced almonds

Directions

1. In a small bowl, whisk together the olive oil, garlic, tamari, lemon juice, salt, and pepper.
2. Combine the tofu and all vegetables in a large bowl.
3. Pour the marinade sauce from step 1 over the tofu and vegetables and toss until evenly coated. Let salad sit at room temperature for approximately 10 minutes.
4. Garnish with almonds before serving.

Avocado and Onion Salad *Serves 4*

¼ cup olive or grape seed oil
Juice of 1 lemon
2 Tbsp. minced garlic, or chopped
Veggie or sea salt and ground black
    pepper to taste
1–2 Tbsp. Louisiana Hot Sauce

1 sweet onion, sliced diagonally (see
    Appendix A, Tip #8)
2–3 Hass avocados, sliced (see Appendix
    A, Tip #6)
4–6 hearts of palm
¼ cup scallions (green onions)

Directions

1. In a bowl, whisk the oil, lemon juice, garlic, salt, pepper, and hot sauce.

2. Add the onions and mix until well coated. Cover tightly and let sit for approximately 10 minutes.

3. Place sliced onion on a plate in a circular pattern, leaving the center of the plate free. (After onion slices are removed, save the marinade sauce for step 5.)

4. Then, in another layer, place the avocados and the hearts of palm around the onions and sprinkle with lemon juice.

5. Drizzle 2 tablespoons of the marinade sauce over the onions, hearts of palm, and avocados.

6. Pour the remaining sauce in a small serving bowl and place the bowl in the open area of the plate. Garnish with scallions and serve.

WHAT IS GRAPE SEED OIL?

Grape seed oil can be found at health food supermarkets or grocery stores with an organic section. This oil is extracted from the seeds of grapes, typically wine grapes. It has two primary usages: cosmetic and culinary. It is light in color and flavor with a hint of nuttiness and contains beneficial compound such as linoleic acid. Linoleic acid is an unsaturated omega-6 essential fatty acid that is important for good health.

WHAT IS HEART OF PALM?

Heart of palm is a vegetable harvested from the soft core of a palm tree. It is popular with vegetarians, who use it in many of their recipes, including salads. For further information, go to http://www.gourmetsleuth.com/Dictionary/H/Heart-of -Palm-5195.aspx.

Cucumber and Tomato Salad *Serves 4*

2 cucumbers
2 ripe tomatoes, quartered
½ cup olive oil
2 Tbsp. minced garlic

Veggie or sea salt and ground black
   pepper to taste
½ tsp. dill, finely chopped

Directions

1. Peel cucumbers. Run a fork lengthwise on the cucumbers to create ridges, then cut the cucumbers in half lengthwise and remove the seeds with a teaspoon (see Appendix A, Tip #10).

2. Put the two halves together and cut lengthwise down the center so you have 4 long pieces of each cucumber. Then put the long pieces together and cut into medium size chunks.

3. Place the tomatoes and cucumbers in a salad bowl and add olive oil, garlic, salt, pepper, and dill. Mix well.

4. Cover tightly and chill for 15 minutes before serving.

Cucumber and Dill Salad *Serves 4*

2 Tbsp. lemon juice
2–3 tsp. minced garlic
Veggie or sea salt and ground black pepper to taste
2 Tbsp. fresh dill, finely chopped
1 large English or regular cucumber, thinly sliced

Directions

1. In a small bowl whisk ½ cup water with the lemon juice, garlic, salt, pepper, and dill until well mixed.

2. Pour over the cucumbers in a salad bowl.

3. Cover and chill in the refrigerator overnight. Serve with dinner.

> **QUICK TIP**
>
> We recommend peeling the cucumber with a swivel-headed peeler because it has a comfortable grip and is great for all vegetable peeling needs. It is quicker than a knife, safe, and it saves time.

Green Bean Salad With Jerusalem Artichoke   *Serves 4*

½ cup olive oil
2 Tbsp. garlic
1 lb. green beans
1 medium Spanish onion, sliced (see
   Appendix A, Tip #8)
2 vine-ripe tomatoes, quartered

1 cup Jerusalem artichoke, sliced
Juice of 1 lime
1 tsp. fresh oregano, chopped
Veggie or sea salt and ground black
   pepper to taste

Directions

1. Boil 3 cups salted water in a 1-quart saucepan, adding 2 tablespoons of olive oil and 2 tablespoons of garlic.

2. While water is coming to a boil, trim the ends of the beans, if needed.

> **SERVING OPTION**
>
> This bean salad can be served over a bed of chopped romaine lettuce or any other lettuce.

3. Add the beans to the boiling water for 2–3 minutes. Remove from heat, drain, and place in refrigerator for 5 minutes.

4. Place sliced onion in a salad bowl. Add the beans, tomatoes, and artichoke to the bowl.

5. In a small bowl, whisk the olive oil, lime juice, oregano, salt, and pepper together. Pour over the salad and chill for 5 minutes before serving.

Boston Salad With Asparagus and Cranberries   *Serves 4*

1 head Boston lettuce, cut into pieces
4 radishes, thinly sliced
1 jícama, thinly sliced
4–6 asparagus spears, stems trimmed and cut in quarters
½ cup carrots, shredded
¼ cup dried cranberries

Directions

1. Wash lettuce and put in a salad spinner (see Appendix A, Tip #5) to remove the water.

2. Toss all ingredients in a large salad bowl and serve with one of the salad dressings from chapter 5.

Zucchini Salad *Serves 4–6*

½ cup dry adzuki beans
½ cup dry black beans
2 Tbsp. veggie or sea salt
2 medium zucchini, finely chopped
½ cup baby bella mushrooms, sliced
2–4 cups lettuce, chopped (romaine,
    Boston, or Butterhead lettuce)
½ cup scallions (green onions), chopped
½ cup cilantro, chopped

½ cup green or black olives
1 tsp. dill (dried or fresh)
1 cup red or white radishes, thinly sliced
1 cup red or sweet onion, thinly sliced
    (optional)

Directions

1. Soak the beans overnight, and in the morning rinse the beans. Place 2 tablespoons salt in 4–6 cups cold water and bring to a boil. Allow beans to cook until tender. When cooked, drain and set aside until cool for approximately 5–10 minutes, and then place in large bowl.

2. Place all the other ingredients in bowl with the beans and toss.

3. Top with one of the salad dressings from chapter 5 or a simple dressing of lemon juice, olive oil, and veggie salt to taste.

4. Chill for 10 minutes and serve.

> **TIME-SAVING OPTION**
>
> When pressed for time, canned beans may be substituted. Open the cans and place beans in a colander, then rinse the beans under cold water and set aside until the water is drained out. Then follow the directions starting from step 2.

Basil and Tomato Salad *Serves 4*

4 large tomatoes, quartered
1 cup fresh basil, cut into strips
1 fresh bay leaf
2 Tbsp. minced garlic
¼ cup olive oil

4–6 Tbsp. rice Parmesan cheese
  (optional)
Veggie or sea salt and ground black
  pepper to taste
2–4 cups romaine lettuce
4–6 Tbsp. rice mozzarella cheese

Directions

1. Place tomatoes in large bowl.

2. In a small bowl, combine ¾ cup basil, bay leaf, garlic, olive oil, cheese, salt, and pepper together. Pour over tomatoes.

3. Make sure that the ingredients are mixed well. Then serve over a bed of romaine lettuce.

4. Garnish with the remaining basil and rice mozzarella cheese.

Daniel's Waldorf Salad *Serves 4*

6–8 lettuce leaves each from two kinds
  of lettuce (romaine, green or red leaf
  lettuce, Boston, etc.)
2 stalks celery, thinly sliced
2 Gala apples, cored and diced
½ cup seedless grapes, halved
1 cup pineapple, chopped

1 Tbsp. lemon juice
½ cup carrots, julienned
3–4 Tbsp. Vegenaise (mayo substitute)
1 cup walnuts
Veggie or sea salt and ground black
  pepper to taste

Directions

1. Wash lettuce leaves and put in salad spinner (see Appendix A, Tip #5) to remove excess water. Leave them whole or tear into large pieces and place in bowl.

2. Wash and thinly slice the celery, and place it in a separate bowl.

3. Add apples to the bowl with celery.

4. Add remaining ingredients to the bowl with the celery and mix well.

5. When you are ready to serve, scoop a large spoonful onto each lettuce leaf, or serve on chopped lettuce.

Daniel's Cobb Salad *Serves 4*

Any three of your favorite lettuces, such as romaine, green or red leaf lettuce, Boston, etc.

5–6 endive leaves, chopped

2–3 Hass avocados (see Appendix A, Tip #6)

2 stalks celery, chopped

2 cucumbers, peeled and chopped

5 red or white radishes, thinly sliced

¼ cup cilantro, finely chopped

2 tomatoes, diced (see Appendix A, Tip #7)

¼ cup black olives

½ cup radicchio

½ jícama, peeled and sliced

Directions

1. Wash lettuce and endive and put in salad spinner (see Appendix A, Tip #5) to dry. Tear lettuce and toss into a large bowl.

2. Add remaining ingredients and toss.

3. Serve with one of the salad dressings from chapter 5.

MAKE YOUR OWN CROUTONS

After the Daniel fast you may want to use the following recipe to make your own croutons.

- Butter both sides of 4 slices of Ezekiel 4:9 Bread or millet bread with Smart Balance Buttery Spread. Lightly brush some minced garlic on both sides.
- Toast bread in a toaster oven or conventional oven at 450 or 475 degrees for approximately 7–10 minutes or until crispy.
- Immediately stack all 4 slices and dice into small squares. Let it sit until cool.
- Lightly dip into a mixture of olive oil, garlic, salt, pepper, rosemary (optional), and oregano and toss over salad.

Add to salad or spaghetti squash and bake with rice cheese, spinach, mushrooms, etc. (See spaghetti squash recipes in chapter 2.)

Greek Salad *Serves 4*

3 large tomatoes, diced (see Appendix
    A, Tip #7)
1 large Spanish onion, diced (see
    Appendix A, Tip #8)
2 cucumbers, seeded and diced (see
    Appendix A, Tip #10)
1 green pepper, diced
8–10 black olives, sliced

4–6 mushrooms, chopped
Juice of 2 lemons
¼ cup olive oil
1 Tbsp. oregano
2 Tbsp. minced garlic
Veggie or sea salt and ground black
    pepper to taste

Directions

1. Wash and prepare all vegetables and place in a large salad bowl.

2. In a small bowl, whisk lemon juice, olive oil, oregano, garlic, salt, and pepper. Pour over the vegetables in the large bowl. Mix until vegetables are well coated.

3. Cover and marinate in refrigerator for 10 minutes before serving.

Grilled Romaine Lettuce Salad *Serves 4*

1–4 hearts of romaine lettuce
¼ cup olive oil
2 Tbsp. garlic

Veggie or sea salt and ground black
    pepper to taste

Directions

1. Preheat oven to 400 degrees.

2. Cut off the heads of the romaine lettuce and discard. Cut the lettuce in half lengthwise. Wash each half and put in a salad spinner (see Appendix A, Tip #5) to remove all water.

3. In a separate bowl, whisk the oil, garlic, salt, and pepper. Dip or rub the mixture on each romaine lettuce half.

4. Place each lettuce half face down on a baking sheet and bake for approximately 5–7 minutes. Remove from oven.

5. Spray a grill pan (see Appendix A, Tip #4) with cooking spray and heat on the stove over high heat. When pan is heated, place the lettuce halves on the grill pan, face down, until each one has the grill imprint, and remove from pan.

6. Serve with the Lemon-Mustard Dressing from chapter 5.

Daniel's Ensalada *Serves 4*

1 head Bibb lettuce or Boston lettuce
3 Tbsp. onion, diced
3 stalks celery, diced
4 red radishes, diced
1 large red bell pepper, diced
½ cup mushrooms, diced
1 cucumber, diced
1 small jícama, peeled and diced
2 cups scallions (green onions)
1½ cups broccoli florets
1½ cups cauliflower florets

1 pint cherry tomatoes
2 Tbsp. red pimiento, minced
1½ cups olive oil
2 Tbsp. Bragg Liquid Aminos
2 Tbsp. minced garlic
1 tsp. veggie or sea salt
1 tsp. paprika
½ tsp. each thyme, basil, oregano,
    marjoram, chervil, and parsley
¼ cup lemon juice

Directions

1. Wash lettuce, dry in a salad spinner (see Appendix A, Tip #5), and separate leaves into bite-size pieces. Place into a serving bowl.

2. Add diced onions, celery, radishes, bell pepper, mushrooms, cucumber, and jícama to the lettuce.

3. Mix in the remaining vegetables.

4. In a salad dressing shaker or a jar, combine the olive oil, Bragg Liquid Aminos, minced garlic, salt, paprika, thyme, basil, oregano, marjoram, chervil, parsley, and lemon juice.

5. Shake and pour generously over the salad.

Chinese Cabbage Salad With Apples and Coarse Black Pepper *Serves 4–6*

1 Chinese cabbage
2 Gala apples, sliced diagonally
2 Tbsp. coarse ground black pepper
2–3 Tbsp. Vegenaise (mayo substitute)
Veggie or sea salt to taste

Directions

1. Wash the cabbage and apples. Tear cabbage into bite-sized pieces and put in a salad spinner (see Appendix A, Tip #5) to dry. Transfer to salad bowl.

2. Cut the apples in half and remove the core, then thinly slice on a diagonal. Add apple slices to cabbage.

3. Add pepper and Vegenaise. Season with salt to taste and mix together until well coated.

> ### VEGENAISE-FREE OPTION
> If you don't want a creamy base to this salad, you can substitute Vegenaise with one of the salad dressings from chapter 5 to complement this simple dish.

Boston Fruit Salad *Serves 6–8*

3 cups fresh strawberries, halved
2 cups green apples, cored and diced
2 cups Gala apples, cored and diced
2 cups seedless grapes, halved
3 kiwi, peeled and sliced
1 cup blueberries

1 cup blackberries
Juice of 4 lemons
½ tsp. vanilla extract
2 Tbsp. maple syrup
4 mint leaves
4 cups Boston lettuce

Directions

1. In a large bowl, combine all the fruit. Set aside.

2. In a small bowl, combine the lemon juice, vanilla extract, maple syrup, and mint leaves. Mix well.

3. Serve fruit over a bed of Boston lettuce. Drizzle with the mint sauce.

Lemon Grilled Tofu
With Tarragon and Dill *Serves 4*

¼ cup olive oil
1 Tbsp. minced garlic
Juice of 2 lemons
Veggie or sea salt and ground black
 pepper to taste
2 16-oz. packs firm tofu, cut into bite-
 sized cubes

½ cup Vegenaise (mayo substitute)
2 Tbsp. of chopped fresh tarragon
2 Tbsp. of chopped fresh dill
1 cup seedless red grapes, halved
½ cup chopped cilantro

Directions

1. Heat an indoor grill or stovetop grill pan (see Appendix A, Tip #4) to 400 degrees.

2. In a bowl, whisk olive oil, garlic, lemon juice, salt, and pepper. Then add the tofu and mix well. Cover and let marinate for at least 10–15 minutes before grilling.

3. In another bowl add the Vegenaise. Fold in the tarragon and dill; season with salt and pepper to taste. Set aside.

4. When grill is heated up to 400 degrees, place the cubed tofu on the grill for 1–2 minutes, and then place tofu on paper towel to absorb any leftover oil.

5. When tofu is cool, transfer to the bowl with the Vegenaise mixture. Add grapes and toss until all ingredients are evenly coated.

6. Refrigerate until ready to serve.

7. Garnish with cilantro and serve over lettuce.

Cabbage Salad *Serves 4*

4 cups green cabbage, shredded
3 cups red cabbage, shredded
½ cup green onions, thinly sliced
1 red bell pepper, seeded and diced
½ red onion, thinly sliced (see Appendix
    A, Tip #8)
½ cup cilantro
Juice of ½ lemon

1 Tbsp. minced garlic
½ cup tamari sauce
½ cup Bragg Liquid Aminos
1 Tbsp. fresh oregano
1 tsp. cumin
Veggie or sea salt and ground black
    pepper to taste

Directions

1. Put the cabbage, green onions, bell pepper, red onion, and cilantro in a large bowl.

2. In a separate bowl, add lemon juice, minced garlic, tamari sauce, Bragg Liquid Aminos, oregano, cumin, and salt and pepper to taste.

3. Add the lemon mixture to the cabbage and mix well.

4. Refrigerate for at least 4–5 hours before serving.

Jícama Salad *Serves 4*

3 jícama, peeled and sliced
2 avocados, peeled and sliced
¼ cup walnuts, chopped

4 artichoke hearts, cut in half
¼ cup dried cranberries
1 red apple, cored and diced

Directions

1. In a large bowl, combine all ingredients.

2. Serve with one of the salad dressings in chapter 5.

Chapter 4

Soups

It is better to eat soup with someone you love...
—Proverbs 15:17, TLB

Pumpkin-Leek Soup *Serves 6–8*

1½ lbs. pumpkin (or calabaza)
3 cups vegetable broth
1 cup water
1 cup leek, chopped
½ tsp. thyme
Veggie or sea salt and ground black pepper
   to taste

PUMPKIN SUBSTITUTE

We use a large calabaza squash as a substitute for the pumpkin in this recipe. You cannot substitute canned pure pumpkin because the consistency is different, and it produces a different texture.

Directions

1. Remove the seeds and rind from the pumpkin (see Appendix A, Tip #1). Cut into small pieces.

2. Place the pumpkin in a pot with 4 cups salted water and bring to a boil. When the pumpkin is fork-tender (see Appendix A, Tip #2), remove from heat and drain.

3. In a separate pot combine the vegetable broth, water, leek, thyme, salt, and pepper. Bring to boil and cook until the leek is tender.

4. Stir pumpkin into vegetable broth mixture. Reduce heat to low, and simmer for 20–30 minutes.

Lentil Soup *Serves 8*

1 package dried lentils (red or green)
4 cups vegetable broth
3 cups cold water
2 Tbsp. kosher salt
6–8 Tbsp. minced garlic
1 cup leek, finely chopped
1 cup fennel, thinly sliced
4–6 celery stalks, chopped
1 sweet onion, chopped (see Appendix A, Tip #8)
2 ripe tomatoes, seeded and chopped (see Appendix A, Tip #7)

2–4 yellow squashes, chopped
2–4 zucchini, chopped
1 cup scallions (green onions), sliced thinly
3 bay leaves
1 cup cilantro, chopped
3 cups pumpkin or calabaza, cooked and chopped (see Appendix A, Tip #1)
Veggie or sea salt and ground black pepper to taste
Juice of 1 lemon

Directions

1. Soak the lentils in warm water overnight, rinse the next morning, and put into a large pot. (This process allows you to remove little stones and other bits of nature that usually end up in the package.)

2. Add vegetable broth, water, and kosher salt to the pot, and bring to a boil. While the lentils are boiling, chop the other vegetables.

3. After the lentils have boiled for 45–60 minutes, add the garlic, leek, fennel, celery, onion, tomatoes, yellow squash, zucchini, $^3/_4$ cup scallions, bay leaves, $^3/_4$ cup cilantro, 2 cups pumpkin, salt, and pepper. Return to boiling.

AFTER-THE-FAST TIP

After your Daniel fast is completed, you may want to add ½ brick coconut cream to this soup and serve it over brown rice or black and mahogany rice.

4. Reduce heat, add lemon juice, cover, and simmer for 20 minutes on low heat.

5. Add more salt and pepper if needed, and remove bay leaves before serving.

6. Garnish the soup with remaining scallions, cilantro, and pumpkin.

Yellow Split Pea Soup *Serves 6–8*

1 lb. yellow split peas
4 cups vegetable broth
2–3 cups cold water
2 Tbsp. kosher salt
6–8 Tbsp. minced garlic
1 cup leek, finely chopped
1 cup fennel, thinly sliced
4–6 celery stalks, chopped
1 sweet onion, chopped
  (see Appendix A, Tip #8)
2 tomatoes, seeded and chopped
  (see Appendix A, Tip #7)

2–4 yellow squashes, chopped
2–4 zucchini, chopped
1 cup scallions (green onions), thinly
  sliced
3 bay leaves
1 cup cilantro, chopped
1½ lbs. pumpkin, chopped in large
  pieces (see Appendix A, Tip #1)
Veggie or sea salt and ground black
  pepper to taste
Juice of 1 lemon
1 tsp. raw pumpkin, shredded

Directions

1. Soak the split peas in warm water overnight, rinse the next morning, and put into a large pot. (This process allows you to remove little stones and other bits of nature that usually end up in the package.)

2. Add vegetable broth, water, and salt, and bring to a boil. While the peas are boiling, chop the other vegetables.

> ## "A SPLIT PEA BY ANY OTHER COLOR…"
>
> Besides yellow, split peas come in green, brown, and red. Follow this recipe for split pea soup exactly the same way regardless of which color you select.

3. After the peas have boiled for 45 minutes, add the garlic, leek, fennel, celery, onion, tomatoes, yellow squash, zucchini, ¾ cup scallions, bay leaves, cilantro, pumpkin, and salt and pepper to taste. Return to boiling.

4. Reduce heat, add lemon juice, and cover and simmer for 20 minutes on low heat.

5. Add more salt and pepper if needed, and remove the bay leaves.

6. Transfer the soup to a blender. (You may have to transfer in batches, depending on how much your blender can hold.) Puree until smooth.

7. Serve hot and garnish with scallions and 1 teaspoon of raw pumpkin.

Roasted Pumpkin and Acorn Squash Soup *Serves 6–8*

1½ lbs. pumpkin (or calabaza squash),
    halved and seeded
1 acorn squash, halved and seeded
4 Tbsp. olive oil
⅓ cup celery, chopped
⅓ cup carrots, chopped
4 Tbsp. yellow onion, chopped (see
    Appendix A, Tip #8)
4 cups vegetable broth

¼ cup unsweetened hemp milk, shaken
1½ tsp. fresh lemon juice
Veggie or sea salt and ground black
    pepper to taste
4 Tbsp. roasted pumpkin seeds
    (see "Roasting Pumpkin Seeds" on
    facing page for recipe)

Directions

1. Preheat oven to 300 degrees.
2. Reserve the seeds removed from the pumpkin halves for a garnish.
3. Place pumpkin and squash on a baking pan, cut side down. Add ½ cup water. Bake about 1 hour and 15 minutes, until fork-tender (see Appendix A, Tip #2). Let cool for approximately 10 minutes before removing peels.

> **USING HEMP MILK AS A THICKENING AGENT**
>
> Hemp milk does not ever get to the same consistency as whipping a heavy cream, but it comes close. If you shake hemp milk until it produces a frothy foam, it adds to the substance of the soup in a similar way to adding heavy cream.

4. Heat olive oil in a saucepan over medium heat. Add celery, carrots, and onion. Cook slowly until the onions are soft, about 5 minutes.
5. Scoop flesh from squash and pumpkin, and add to vegetables in saucepan. Add vegetable broth and bring to a boil. Reduce heat, cover, and simmer slowly until the carrots and celery are tender, about 25–30 minutes.
6. Transfer soup to a blender and puree until smooth. Return to pan and add milk, lemon juice, salt, and pepper.
7. When soup is heated through, transfer to serving bowls and garnish with roasted pumpkin seeds.

Vegetable Soup *Serves 4–6*

¼ cup olive oil
4–6 Tbsp. minced garlic
1 yellow onion, chopped (see Appendix A, Tip #8)
1 sweet onion, chopped
4–6 stalks of celery, sliced
2 medium carrots, sliced
1 head cabbage, shredded
2 medium zucchini, cut into ¼-inch chunks
1 cup leek, finely sliced

1 cup fennel, finely sliced
2 tomatoes, chopped
1 lb. fresh green beans
4–6 cups vegetable broth
Veggie or sea salt and ground black pepper to taste
1 28-oz. can whole tomatoes (do not drain)
1 can pinto beans, washed and drained

Directions

1. In a large pot over high heat, heat the olive oil. Add the garlic, onions, celery, carrots, cabbage, zucchini, leek, fennel, tomatoes, and green beans. Sauté until vegetables are tender, stirring constantly.

2. Add the vegetable broth, 2 cups water, salt, and pepper, and bring to a boil.

3. Add the can of tomatoes (with the liquid) and pinto beans. Reduce heat to low, and cover and simmer for 25–30 minutes. Taste to determine if additional salt and pepper are needed before serving.

ROASTING PUMPKIN SEEDS

- Remove seeds from the pumpkin, rinse pumpkin seeds under cold water, picking out the pulp and strings.
- Place the pumpkin seeds in a single layer on a baking sheet with olive oil. Stir seeds until they are coated with olive oil. If you prefer, you can spray the pumpkin seeds with a nonstick cooking spray instead of using olive oil.
- Sprinkle pumpkin seeds with sea salt or veggie salt, and bake at 325 degrees until toasted, about 25 minutes, and stirring after 10 minutes.

Vegetable Gumbo *Serves 6*

¼ cup olive oil
3–6 Tbsp. minced garlic (or crushed)
1 large sweet onion, diced (see Appendix A, Tip #8)
1 large green bell pepper, diced
¼ tsp. thyme
Veggie or sea salt and ground black pepper to taste
2–4 Tbsp. Creole seasoning, to taste

4 cups vegetable broth
1 15-oz. can pinto beans, drained and rinsed
1 16-oz. can tomatoes
1 10-oz. bag frozen okra, sliced
4–6 green bananas in their peels
1 yuca root, peeled
2 white yams, peeled
½ cup scallions (green onions), chopped

Directions

1. Heat oil in a large pot over medium-high heat. Add garlic, onion, bell pepper, thyme, salt, pepper, and desired amount of Creole seasoning, stirring constantly until the garlic turns golden brown.

2. Add the vegetable broth, pinto beans, tomatoes, and frozen okra. Cover and simmer for approximately 30 minutes.

3. In a separate pot, add 4–6 cups cold water with salt. Add the green bananas (with peels) and bring to boil. When the banana peels split open, they are cooked. Drain water and let cool for approximately 10 minutes before removing the peels.

4. In a separate pot, add salt to 4–6 cups cold water. Add the yuca and yams, and bring to a boil. When they are fork-tender (see Appendix A, Tip #2), remove from heat and drain. Let cool for 10 minutes.

5. Dice the bananas and yuca root and slice the yams. Add all three vegetables to the pot with the okra mixture. Stir all ingredients together.

6. Transfer to serving bowls and garnish with scallions.

> **SEASONING RECOMMENDATION**
>
> We recommend Konriko Creole Seasoning because it is wheat and gluten free and contains no MSG. For more information, visit their website at www.konriko.com.

Cannellini Bean Soup With Kale *Serves 4*

1 lb. dried cannellini beans
1 bunch rainbow kale (or green kale)
¼ cup olive oil
3–6 Tbsp. crushed garlic
1 sweet onion, chopped (see Appendix A, Tip #8)
4 stalks celery, chopped
4–6 tomatoes, seeded and diced (see Appendix A, Tip #7)
3 bay leaves
½ cup leek, chopped
½ cup fennel, chopped

2 Tbsp. dry oregano
½ cup dried chili flakes
4 cups vegetable broth
¼ cup Bragg Liquid Aminos
½ cup parsley, chopped
½ cup fresh basil, chopped
1 cup cilantro, chopped
1 cup scallions (green onions), chopped
Veggie or sea salt and ground black pepper to taste
1 tsp. calabaza squash, shredded

Directions

1. Soak the beans overnight. Drain and rinse the beans, transfer them to a large pot with 4–6 cups cold, salted water, and bring to boil. Remove any froth from the surface. Uncover pot, reduce heat, and simmer.

2. While the beans are simmering, rinse each kale leaf, chop, and set aside.

3. In a saucepan, heat the olive oil over medium heat. Add the garlic and stir until it gets golden. Then add onions, celery, tomatoes, bay leaves, leek, fennel, oregano, and chili flakes. Stir for 5–7 minutes or until the vegetables are fork-tender (see Appendix A, Tip #2).

4. When beans are tender, add the vegetable broth and Bragg Liquid Aminos. Transfer the mixture in the saucepan to the pot. Add the parsley, basil, ¾ cup cilantro, ¾ cup scallions, and salt and pepper to taste and stir. Bring to a boil.

5. Reduce heat, add kale, and let simmer uncovered for 8–10 minutes. Allow the broth to thicken. Season with more salt and pepper if needed.

6. Serve hot and garnish with the remaining cilantro, scallions, and squash.

Black Bean Soup *Serves 4–6*

1 lb. dry black beans
4 cups vegetable broth
1 cup leek, chopped
1 cup fennel, chopped
1 sweet onion, chopped (see Appendix A, Tip #8)
1 yellow onion, chopped
1 red onion, chopped

1 cup cilantro, chopped
1 cup scallions (green onions), chopped
½ tsp. thyme
1 Tbsp. paprika
Veggie or sea salt and ground black pepper to taste
3 bay leaves

Directions

1. Soak beans in warm water overnight. Drain and rinse the beans, and transfer them to a large pot with vegetable broth and 2 cups cold, salted water. Bring to boil.

2. While the beans are cooking, chop leek, fennel, onions, cilantro, and scallions. Set aside ¼ cup red onion for garnishing.

3. Sauté leek, fennel, onions, cilantro, scallions, thyme, and paprika for 1 minute. Then season with salt and pepper to taste.

4. Add bay leaves and all other ingredients to boiling beans and simmer, covered, for approximately 20–30 minutes.

5. Remove bay leaves before serving. Garnish with red onions.

WHY DO BAY LEAVES HAVE TO BE REMOVED?

Bay leaves remain stiff even after cooking, so to avoid accidental swallowing whole or in large pieces, which may scratch the digestive tract or cause choking, it is recommended that you remove the bay leaf after cooking.

Broccoli Soup *Serves 4–6*

¾ cup vegetable broth
1–2 cups frozen broccoli or broccoli
   florets
2 Tbsp. olive oil
1 small sweet onion, chopped
   (see Appendix A, Tip #8)

1–2 Tbsp. minced garlic (or chopped)
1 cup hemp milk
2 cups rice cheddar cheese
Veggie or sea salt and ground black
   pepper to taste

Directions

1. Heat vegetable broth in a pot over high heat. Add the broccoli florets. When it comes to a boil, stir, and promptly remove from heat.

2. In a saucepan, heat olive oil over high heat and sauté onion and garlic until the garlic is slightly golden.

3. Add the ingredients in the saucepan to the pot with the broccoli florets, then add the milk. Stir until blended.

4. Transfer 2–3 cups of the mixture to the blender and purée. Hold the lid firmly and cover the lid with a paper towel in order to prevent splashing or burning. Continue the process until all of the broccoli mixture is puréed. Then transfer the mixture back to the pot, and stir until it is hot. Remove from heat. Add 1½ cups cheese to the mixture, stirring until dissolved.

5. Top with remaining cheese just before serving.

Zucchini and Pumpkin Soup *Serves 4–6*

2 cups vegetable broth
1 lb. pumpkin, peeled and chopped into
   small/medium size pieces
   (see Appendix A, Tip #1)
4 medium zucchini, chopped
2 onions, chopped
   (see Appendix A, Tip #8)

6 Tbsp. minced garlic
4 stalks celery, chopped
Veggie or sea salt and ground black
   pepper to taste
¾ cup Vegenaise (mayo substitute)
Juice of 1–2 lemons
¼ tsp. nutmeg or cinnamon

Directions

1. Heat vegetable broth with 4–6 cups cold water in a large pot; add pumpkin. Boil over high heat for approximately 15–20 minutes or until fork-tender (see Appendix A, Tip #2).

2. Add the zucchini, onions, garlic, and celery. Cook for approximately 15 minutes. Add salt and pepper to taste. Cover and simmer for another 5–10 minutes on low heat.

3. Puree the mixture in a food processor or blender, adding the Vegenaise, lemon juice, and nutmeg or cinnamon.

4. Transfer to serving bowls. This soup can be served hot or cold.

Bean Soup *Serves 4–6*

½ cup dry pinto beans
½ cup dry black beans
½ cup dry adzuki beans
4 cups vegetable broth
1 lb. pumpkin or calabaza squash,
    chopped (see Appendix A, Tip #1)
¼ cup olive oil
4–6 Tbsp. minced garlic (or chopped)
1 sweet onion, finely chopped (see
    Appendix A, Tip #8)
1 yellow onion, finely chopped
1 red onion, finely chopped

1 cup cilantro, chopped
½ tsp. thyme
½ cup scallions (green onions), chopped
1 cup leek, chopped
½ cup fennel, chopped
1 zucchini, chopped
Veggie or sea salt and ground black
    pepper to taste
½ tsp. paprika
1–2 tsp. cumin
3 bay leaves

Directions

1. Soak beans in warm water overnight.
    Drain and rinse beans, place in large
    pot with vegetable broth and 3 cups
    salted water, and bring to a boil.

2. While the beans are cooking, remove
    the skin and seeds from the pumpkin
    (see Appendix A, Tip #1), and cut
    into 1-inch chunks. Then add the
    pumpkin chunks to the beans.

3. In a separate pan, heat the olive oil
    over high heat and sauté the garlic,
    onions, cilantro, thyme, scallions, leek,
    fennel, and zucchini for 1 minute.
    Season with salt and pepper to taste.

4. Check the tenderness of the
    pumpkin. If fork-tender (see
    Appendix A, Tip #2) add all the other
    ingredients, cover, and bring to a boil.

5. Remove bay leaves and garnish with
    red onions before serving.

TIPS FOR AVOIDING GAS FROM BEANS

Gas can be caused by several things,
such as chewing food with your mouth
open, eating too fast, and eating
certain types of sugars, fiber, and
starch. The following foods cause
gas: beans, milk and dairy products
(especially if you're lactose intolerant),
and sugar, including sorbitol and
fructose. Sorbitol is found in artificial
sweetening agents, so try and avoid
sugar-free products. Starches such as
potatoes and pasta also produce gas,
but while on the Daniel fast you'll be
avoiding these completely. Oat bran,
peas, and some fruit also produce
gas. To avoid gas, try to limit the
your intake of those foods that you
know cause excessive gas. Chew your
food slowly with your mouth closed.
Beano is an over-the-counter product
that may help (check with your doctor
before taking any medication), as it
helps in breaking down starches and
relieves gas produced by these foods.
Activated charcoal tabs may also help.

Pinto, Adzuki, and Bok Choy Soup *Serves 4–6*

½ pound dry pinto beans
½ pound dry adzuki beans
½ cup olive oil
2 small carrots, diced
1 shallot, chopped
1 large tomato, diced
  (see Appendix A, Tip #7)
2 Tbsp. minced garlic

1 stalk celery
4 cups kale, chopped
1 large turnip, diced
2 cups bok choy, chopped
2 tsp. dill, minced
1 tsp. cilantro, chopped
Veggie or sea salt and ground black
  pepper to taste

Directions

1. Soak beans in warm water overnight. Drain and rinse beans, and put them in a pot. Cover with 6–8 cups water and bring to boil.

2. Reduce heat and simmer until beans are fork-tender (see Appendix A, Tip #2), about 1½ hours.

3. Spoon the beans with a slotted spoon into a food processor or blender and puree. Reserve the bean liquid that remains in the pot for later.

4. Heat olive oil in a saucepan over high heat, adding carrots, shallot, diced tomatoes, garlic, and celery. Stir for 5 minutes.

5. Add kale, turnip, bean puree, bok choy, dill, cilantro, and salt and pepper to taste in to the pot with the bean liquid.

6. Add the ingredients in the saucepan to the pot and stir, adding salt and pepper to taste. Cover and simmer over medium heat for 30 minutes.

> ### WHAT ARE ADZUKI BEANS?
>
> Adzuki beans are small, dark red/brown oval beans approximately 5 millimeters in diameter with a distinctive white ridge along one side. Adzuki beans are popular across Asia, particularly in Japan, and are used to make a red sweet bean paste. In the Far East it is often known as the "Mercedes" of beans, where it is principally used, after fermentation, as a confectionery product.

> ### WHAT IS BOK CHOY?
>
> Bok choy is a vegetable that resembles celery, although is actually a member of the cabbage family. It has thick white stalks and dark green leaves that have a round shape. Both the stalks and leaves are edible. Baby bok choy can be enjoyed cooked or raw. It can also be used in salads.

Cabbage Vegetable Soup *Serves 6–8*

4 cups vegetable broth
2–3 cups cold water
1 head cabbage, thinly shredded
4 Tbsp. minced garlic
Veggie or sea salt and ground black
 pepper to taste
2–4 tomatoes, cubed
½ cup leek, chopped

½ cup fennel, chopped
½ cup cilantro, chopped
½ cup carrots, cubed
1 zucchini, diced or cubed
Juice of 1 lemon
½ tsp. red crushed pepper (more or less,
 to taste)
1 package frozen green beans

Directions

1. In a large pot, combine the vegetable broth, 2–3 cups water, cabbage, garlic, salt, and pepper, and bring to a boil.

2. When the cabbage is slightly tender, add the tomatoes, leek, fennel, cilantro, and carrots. Add more salt and pepper if needed. Cover and return to boiling. Reduce heat and simmer for another 30 minutes.

3. Add the zucchini, lemon juice, and red crushed pepper, and beans. Simmer for another 10 minutes. Remove from heat, stir, and serve. (The zucchini should be a little crunchy when served.)

Pumpkin and Yellow Pepper Soup *Serves 6–8*

1½ lb. pumpkin (or calabaza squash)
4–8 cups vegetable broth
1 yellow onion, diced
  (see Appendix A, Tip #8)
3 stalks celery, cut in ½-inch pieces
4–6 Tbsp. minced garlic
1 cup cilantro, chopped
½ cup leek, chopped
½ cup fennel, chopped
8 yellow bell peppers, seeded and
  chopped

½ cup fresh parsley
2–4 ripe tomatoes, crushed
½ cup scallions (green onions), chopped
1 carrot, peeled
Veggie or sea salt and ground black
  pepper to taste
1 Tbsp. fresh thyme
2 Tbsp. juice from a lemon

Directions

1. Cut the pumpkin in half, remove the skin and seeds (see Appendix A, Tip #1), and chop into large chunks. Place the pumpkin chunks in a pot with the vegetable broth over high heat.

2. Add the onion, celery, garlic, cilantro, leek, fennel, bell peppers, parsley, tomatoes, scallions, carrot, salt, and pepper. Bring to a boil.

3. When peppers are tender, reduce heat and simmer for approximately 35–45 minutes.

4. Spoon some of the vegetables into a food processor or blender. (Be careful because they will be hot.) Cover the mouth of the blender with a paper towel or kitchen towel in case the liquid splatters. Puree the ingredients and place in a separate bowl. Repeat the process until all the vegetables have been pureed.

5. Return all of the ingredients to the pot. Add the thyme and 2 tablespoons of lemon juice. Mix well and simmer on low heat for approximately 10–15 minutes.

6. Add more seasoning if needed. Garnish with cilantro, and serve.

Zucchini Soup *Serves 4*

1 carton vegetable broth
4 medium zucchini, sliced
2 medium onions, chopped
3 Tbsp. minced garlic
Veggie or sea salt to taste

¼ cup cilantro, chopped
1 cup Vegenaise (mayo substitute)
2 tsp. lemon juice
¼ tsp. ground nutmeg
Lemon slices for garnish

Directions

1. In a saucepan, bring the vegetable broth, zucchini, onions, garlic, and salt to a boil. Cook for approximately 10 minutes or until vegetables are fork-tender (see Appendix A, Tip #2).
2. Remove from heat. Place half of mixture at a time in the blender and purée. Transfer to a large bowl and stir in the remaining ingredients. (Reserve a small amount of cilantro for garnish.)
3. Cover and chill overnight. Garnish with lemon slices and cilantro.

Tomato Bisque *Serves 4–6*

2 Tbsp. olive oil
2 medium onions, chopped
2 Tbsp. minced garlic
6 large tomatoes, peeled and cubed
1 cup water
1–2 vegetable bouillon cubes
2¼ tsp. fresh dill (or ¾ tsp. dried)
1 Tbsp. cilantro

Veggie or sea salt and ground black
    pepper to taste
½ cup Vegenaise (mayo substitute)
1 tomato, sliced, for garnish
Dill sprigs for garnish

Directions

1. In a medium saucepan, heat the olive oil over medium heat. Add onions and garlic and sauté until tender.
2. Add water, tomatoes, bouillon, dill, cilantro, and salt and pepper to taste. Cover and simmer for approximately 10–15 minutes.
3. Remove from heat and let cool. Add half at a time to a blender and purée. Transfer to a large bowl and stir in the Vegenaise, salt, and pepper.
4. Cover and chill overnight. When serving, garnish with sliced tomatoes and dill sprigs.

Pumpkin Bisque *Serves 6–8*

2 cups water
Veggie or sea salt to taste
8 lb. pumpkin or calabaza, peeled, cut
    in large pieces with seeds and pulp
    removed
2 cups vegetable broth
1 onion, finely chopped
¼ cup green onions, thinly sliced
¼ tsp. nutmeg

⅛ tsp. fresh ginger, grated
2 Tbsp. minced garlic
1 tsp. Season-All
3 Tbsp. chives
Ground black pepper to taste
1 stick cinnamon
2 cups hemp milk
1 cup Vegenaise (mayo substitute)

Directions

1. In a large pot over high heat, add water, salt, and pumpkin. Cover and bring to a boil. Lower heat and simmer uncovered for approximately 20–30 minutes or until fork-tender (see Appendix A, Tip #2).

> **QUICK TIP**
>
> If pressed for time, use two or three 16-oz. cans of pumpkin (not the pumpkin used to make pumpkin pies) and follow the directions above.

2. Add vegetable broth, onion, green onions, nutmeg, ginger, minced garlic, Season-All, 2 tablespoons chives, and salt and pepper to taste. Cook uncovered for approximately 10-15 minutes.

3. Remove from heat and place ingredients in blender. Purée until smooth.

4. Return to heat. Add cinnamon stick and bring to boil.

5. Blend milk and Vegenaise in blender until smooth.

6. Remove soup from heat. Add milk mixture and mix well.

7. Garnish with chives and serve.

Chapter 5

Salad Dressings, Marinades, and Sauces

...pouring oil and wine on them...
—Luke 10:34

Lemon-Garlic Dressing *Makes 6–8 servings (1–2 Tbsp. per serving)*

4 lemons
½ cup olive oil
2 Tbsp. minced garlic
¼ tsp. of dill
Veggie or sea salt and ground black pepper to taste

Directions

1. Juice lemons by cutting them in half and squeezing the juice into a strainer over a bowl. The juice should flow through the strainer and collect in the bowl.

2. Add olive oil, garlic, dill, salt, and pepper. Whisk with a wire whisk and serve over salad immediately.

> **Quick Tip**
>
> Try this recipe with limes instead of lemons for a nice change of pace.

Bragg Liquid Aminos Dressing *Makes 6–8 servings (2 Tbsp. per serving)*

1 lemon (or lime)
¼ cup Bragg Liquid Aminos
½ cup olive oil
2–3 Tbsp. minced garlic
1 Tbsp. finely chopped cilantro
Veggie or sea salt and ground black pepper to taste

Directions

1. Juice lemon by cutting in half and squeezing the juice into a strainer over a bowl. The juice should flow through the strainer and collect in the bowl.

2. Add Bragg Liquid Aminos, olive oil, garlic, cilantro, salt, and pepper. Whisk with a wire whisk and serve over salad immediately.

> **Quick Tip**
>
> You can use Bragg Liquid Aminos any time you are marinating or sautéing veggies.

Lemon or Lime Dressing *Makes 6 servings (2 Tbsp. per serving)*

1–2 lemons (or lime)
½ cup olive oil
1 Tbsp. minced garlic
Veggie or sea salt and ground black pepper to taste
2 slices of ginger

Directions

1. Juice lemon or lime by cutting in half and squeezing the juice into a strainer over a bowl. The juice should flow through the strainer and collect in the bowl.

2. Add olive oil, garlic, salt, and pepper. Whisk with a wire whisk, then add ginger and serve over salad immediately.

> **WE RECOMMEND**
>
> Use our alternative dressings and stay away from sugary, chemical-laden store-bought salad dressings. You'll not only taste the difference, but you'll also *feel* the difference!

Lemon-Mustard Dressing *Makes 4–6 servings (2 Tbsp. per serving)*

Juice of 1 lemon
1 tsp. fresh chives, chopped
¾ cup olive oil
1 tsp. dry mustard
¼ cup Bragg Liquid Aminos
Veggie or sea salt and ground black pepper to taste

Directions

1. Juice lemon by cutting in half and squeezing the juice into a strainer over a bowl. The juice should flow through the strainer and collect in the bowl.

2. Add chives, olive oil, dry mustard, Bragg Liquid Aminos, salt, and pepper. Whisk with a wire whisk and serve over salad immediately.

Cilantro-Garlic Dressing *Makes 6 servings (2 Tbsp. per serving)*

2 lemons
½ cup olive oil
½ cup Bragg Liquid Aminos
½ cup tamari sauce
½ cup cilantro
3–4 Tbsp. minced garlic (or more, if preferred)

4–8 slices fresh ginger
½ cup scallions (green onions), finely chopped
½ tsp. dill
Veggie or sea salt and ground black pepper to taste

Directions

1. Juice lemons by cutting in half and squeezing the juice into a strainer over a bowl. The juice should flow through the strainer and collect in the bowl.
2. Add olive oil, Bragg Liquid Aminos, tamari sauce, cilantro, garlic, ginger, scallions, dill, salt, and pepper. Whisk with a wire whisk and serve over salad immediately.

Tahini Salad Dressing *Makes 6 servings (2 Tbsp. per serving)*

Juice of 2 lemons
3–4 Tbsp. tahini sauce
2–3 Tbsp. minced garlic

½ cup olive oil
Veggie or sea salt and ground black pepper to taste

Directions

1. Juice lemons by cutting in half and squeezing the juice into a strainer over a bowl. The juice should flow through the strainer and collect in the bowl.
2. Add tahini sauce, garlic, olive oil, salt, and pepper. Whisk with a wire whisk and serve over salad immediately.

Garlic Dressing *Makes 6 servings (2 Tbsp. per serving)*

3 Tbsp. minced garlic
3 Tbsp. cilantro, chopped
1 Tbsp. fresh squeezed lemon juice
3 Tbsp. hemp milk

1 cup of Vegenaise (mayo substitute)
2 Tbsp. Bragg Liquid Aminos
Veggie or sea salt and ground black pepper to taste

Directions

1. Place all ingredients in a bowl and mix well, or add to a blender and blend.
2. Cover and chill for 20 minutes, and then serve over fresh salad.

Marinade Sauce *Makes 1–2 cups*

½ cup tamari sauce
½ cup Bragg Liquid Aminos
½ cup organic brown sugar
½ cup scallions (green onions)
¼ cup thinly sliced ginger

Directions

SUGGESTED USES

We use this marinade sauce for fish, chicken, or beef. Marinate overnight for a better flavor. We use a George Foreman grill to cook the meats.

1. Combine all ingredients in a large bowl.
   (Preferably, you should use a bowl with an airtight lid, but if you don't have one, you can seal the bowl with plastic wrap instead.)

2. Add whatever meat or fish you are marinating and mix until meat is well coated. I usually use approximately 2–3 pounds of meat or fish.

3. Cover tightly and refrigerate overnight.

4. The next day, remove the meat and cook accordingly.

Teriyaki Sauce *Makes 1–2 cups*

½ cup tamari sauce
½ cup Bragg Liquid Aminos
½ cup maple syrup
¼ cup sliced ginger
½ cup scallions (green onions), sliced

DURING- AND AFTER-THE-FAST TIPS

We use this sauce to stir-fry vegetables. When you are not on the Daniel fast, use this sauce with salmon, meat, or noodle dishes. This sauce can be used immediately or refrigerated and used whenever desired. It can last approximately two months.

Directions

1. Combine all ingredients in a pot and stir constantly over high heat.

2. Bring to boil, continuing to stir constantly until sauce thickens.

3. This sauce can be used immediately over meats, fish, noodles, or stir-fry vegetables. It can also be stored, preferably in a glass jar, by cooling for approximately 10–15 minutes before covering and refrigerating for future use.

Mango Chutney *Makes 1–2 cups*

1 mango, diced
1 cucumber, seeded and cubed
   (see Appendix A, Tip #10)
Juice of 1 lime
2–4 Tbsp. olive oil
¼ cup fresh basil, chopped
¼ cup cilantro
2 tsp. jalapeño peppers, chopped
¼ cup scallions (green onions), chopped
½ tsp. sea salt
Black pepper to taste

> **AFTER-THE-FAST TIP**
>
> After the Daniel fast, this chutney can be used on fish, chicken, or lamb.

Directions

1. Combine all ingredients in a blender or food processor and chop for approximately 5–7 minutes. (For chunkier consistency, wait until blending is completed before adding the mango.)

2. Transfer to a bowl, cover, and refrigerate for approximately 10–15 minutes or overnight.

> **PEELING AND DICING MANGOS**
>
> Mangoes are very slippery and can present a challenge when peeling, so you have to be very careful. Instead of removing the peel with a knife or peeler, we usually leave the peel on and start by cutting through the mango lengthwise on either side of the pit with a serrated (jagged-edged) knife.
>
> Once the pit is removed, we use a paring knife to score the flesh of the mango lengthwise, diagonally, about 1/2 inch thick. Then we press the backside of the mango (the peel side) so that all the flesh stands out, making it easier to trim away the flesh from the peel. Then we remove all of the sliced flesh from the peel and dice.

Papaya Chutney *Makes 1–2 cups*

2 green papayas
    (see Appendix A, Tip #9)
2 large yellow Spanish onions, quartered
    (see Appendix A, Tip #8)
2 Tbsp. garlic

1 bunch Spanish thyme
¼ tsp. sea salt
½ cup white or apple cider vinegar
Veggie or sea salt and ground black
    pepper to taste

Directions

1. Peel the papayas, cut in half, and scoop out the seeds with a spoon. Then cut the papayas into quarters. Place in pot with at least 4–5 cups salted water (enough to cover the papaya quarters).

2. Bring to a boil. When papaya is fork-tender (see Appendix A, Tip #2), drain it and place it on a plate.

3. Blend onions, garlic, thyme, sea salt, vinegar, and ¼ cup water in a food processor or blender until well mixed.

4. Reserve a few diced papaya pieces and place the remaining papaya in the food processor. Blend the ingredients and then stir to make sure all the ingredients are well mixed. The mixture should be smooth like yogurt. Then add the reserved diced papayas back to this mixture.

5. Season with salt and pepper.

> **QUICK TIPS**
>
> • Chutney can be used in soups as well as in cooking meats or rice. It is also great to eat along with any meal or mangoes, cantaloupe, melon, etc. It heightens the flavor of foods.
> • This papaya chutney can be stored in the refrigerator for up to three months.

Easy Basil Pesto *Makes 1 cup*

3 Tbsp. minced garlic

2 cups basil

⅓ cup pine nuts

½ cup rice Parmesan cheese

½ cup olive oil

Veggie or sea salt and ground black pepper to taste

Directions

1. Blend first four ingredients together in a blender.

2. While the machine is blending, add the olive oil until well blended.

3. Season with salt and pepper.

Chapter 6

BEVERAGES

I was thirsty, and you gave Me something to drink.
—MATTHEW 25:35

Peach Sun Tea *Serves 6–8*

7 tea bags of Celestial Seasonings Peach Tea (or any other brand of decaffeinated peach tea)
1 tsp. of maple syrup to taste (optional)
4–5 fresh mint leaves (optional)

Directions

1. Put about 7 tea bags into a large clear glass jar or pitcher. Add 6–8 cups cold water.

2. Set the jar in direct sunlight for about 6 hours, checking periodically for the strength of the tea and to make sure it is still in the sun. If you place the jar outside, cover it with plastic wrap or a paper towel to keep out bugs or debris.

3. Bring in from the sun, sweeten with maple syrup (optional), and pour over ice in tall glasses.

4. Garnish with fresh mint leaves (optional).

QUICK TIPS

- This tea tastes good without *any* sugar—and that's better for you!
- Tea brewed in the sun will not be as hot as tea that has been steeped in boiling water. However, it is perfect for iced tea.
- Sun tea is made in the Southern tradition! John's mother handed down this Southern way of making tea from her father's family, who were from Mississippi.

Flavored Waters *Serves 8*

8 tsp. unsweetened cranberry
  or wild blueberry concentrate
Juice of 3–4 lemons
8 10-oz. glasses of cold water
Maple syrup to taste (optional)

Directions

1. Add unsweetened concentrated cranberry or blueberry juice and freshly squeezed lemon juice to a glass of drinking water.

2. Sweeten with maple syrup (optional).

Herbal Teas *Serves 2–4*

Your choice of peppermint, chamomile, mint,
  green tea, apple cinnamon, or other variety of decaffeinated herbal tea
1 tsp. maple syrup or rice milk (optional)

Directions

1. Pour boiling water into a teapot (makes 2–4 cups) or a cup. (Unlike the sun tea recipe in this book, the key with herbal teas is to steep them in very hot water to allow the herbs to infuse their flavors.) Add teabags according to the strength you prefer.

2. Allow tea to steep for 2–5 minutes.

3. Sweeten with maple syrup or rice milk (optional).

> ### TRY FRESH OR DRIED HERBS INSTEAD OF TEABAGS
>
> You can also make herbal tea from fresh or dried herbs. Simply add the loose herbs directly to the boiling water, steep for 1–2 minutes, and strain the tea before serving. A rule of thumb is to use 3 tablespoons of fresh herbs or 1 tablespoon of dried herbs to a pot of tea. (Dried herbs have a stronger flavor than fresh.)

> ### HERBS THAT HEAL
>
> Some great-tasting herbal combinations and their healing properties are:
> - Ginger and peppermint (helps soothe upset stomach)
> - Chamomile and peppermint (helps you relax and fall asleep)
> - Thyme (helps relieve fever and cough)
> - Alfalfa, chamomile, ginger, and willow bark (helps relieve aches and pains)
> - Peppermint, dandelion root, ginger, licorice root, and cayenne pepper (aids in digestive cleansing)

Daniel-Friendly Milk Alternatives *Serves 1*

Hemp, soy, or rice/soy milk
Carob or vanilla (optional)

Directions

1. If you like drinking milk, try rice, hemp, soy, or a combination of rice/soy milk. During the Daniel fast, you can drink milk flavored with carob or vanilla, or just drink it plain. (Stay away from chocolate during the Daniel fast.) Add this to your cereal, tea, or over fruit.

Daniel-Friendly Coffee Alternatives *Serves 1*

Pero; Cafix; naturally caffeine free, nonacidic, gluten-free Teeccino; or Mediterranean herbal coffee (natural coffee alternatives)

Directions

1. You should not have coffee on the Daniel fast, but if you just have to have a cup of coffee, we suggest Pero, Cafix, Teeccino, or Mediterranean herbal coffee. Teeccino can be brewed in your coffeepot, smells wonderful, and is great to wake up to. These coffees can be picked up from Whole Foods Market or your local grocery store in the health food section.

Chapter 7

HEALTHY SNACKS

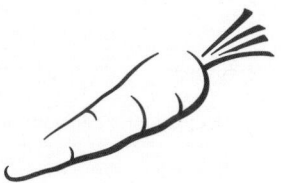

...and be in good health...
—3 JOHN 2

Pumpkin and Carob Mix *Serves 8*

1 lb. raw pumpkin seeds
1 lb. carob

Directions

1. Mix these two together in a plastic bag, and you have yourself a filling and tasty snack when those hunger pangs happen.

Cranberry and Coconut Mix *Serves 8*

1 lb. dried cranberries
1 lb. dried coconut flakes

Directions

1. Mix these two together in a plastic bag for a delicious, wholesome snack.

Walnut Trail Mix *Serves 8*

1 lb. organic raw walnuts
1 lb. dried cranberries
1 lb. raw pumpkin seeds
1 lb. organic raisins

Directions

1. Mix these all together in a plastic bag and dig in when you feel just a bit faint!

Carrot or Celery Sticks and Almond Butter *Serves 8*

8 organic carrot sticks
8 organic celery sticks
Almond butter

Directions

1. Rinse, cover, and set aside the carrot and celery sticks in the fridge for about an hour. Take out and spread with almond butter.

HEALTHY EATING AFTER THE DANIEL FAST

Chapter 8

BREAKFASTS

Jesus said to them, "Come and have breakfast."
—JOHN 21:12

Arroz y Leche (Rice and Milk) *Serves 4*

1 cup brown rice
1 Tbsp. soy margarine or rice butter
½ cup rice, soy, soy/rice, or hemp milk
Cinnamon
Maple syrup (optional)

Directions

1. Cook rice according to package instructions.

2. Transfer some of the rice to a bowl and add a little soy margarine or rice butter. Add rice, soy, soy/rice, or hemp milk.

3. Top with cinnamon.

4. Add maple syrup if extra sweetness is desired.

Quick Tips

- For brown rice, we recommend Texmati—it's our favorite! For information on Texmati rice, visit their website at http://www.riceselect.com/home.aspx.
- This cereal is great for a morning meal or in the middle of the afternoon on a cold day.
- You can use a rice cooker for this recipe if you have one (see Appendix A, Tip #11).
- This is a traditional Mexican meal. It really warms you and fills you. It actually tastes best when you reheat leftover rice from dinner the night before!

Chopped Spinach and Mushroom Omelet *Serves 2*

2 Tbsp. Smart Balance Buttery Spread
½ cup spinach, chopped
½ cup mushrooms, chopped
1 tsp. minced garlic
2 Tbsp. scallions (green onions), thinly
  sliced

Veggie or sea salt and ground black
  pepper to taste
¾ cup egg whites
1 Tbsp. hemp milk
¼ cup rice mozzarella cheese
2 Tbsp. cilantro, chopped

Directions

1. Coat medium skillet with cooking spray before heating over high heat. Add Smart Balance Buttery Spread, spinach, mushrooms, garlic, and scallions. Stir until spinach wilts, approximately 1–2 minutes. Then season with salt and pepper to taste.

> **SERVING TIP**
>
> The omelet can be served with 1 slice of millet toast or toasted Ezekiel 4:9 Cinnamon Bread and organic strawberry preserves. Delicious!

2. Pour spinach mixture into a strainer lined with a paper towel. Use the paper towel to squeeze out all water. Set aside.

3. In a mixing bowl, whisk egg whites and milk.

4. Re-coat the skillet with cooking spray and heat over medium-high heat. Pour egg mixture into skillet and cook. Use a rubber spatula to lift the edge of the egg mixture as it cooks, and tilt the pan to allow any uncooked eggs to drain underneath the cooked portion. This process should take approximately 1 minute.

5. When all egg mixture is cooked, fill the center of the omelet with the vegetable mixture, adding the cheese and cilantro. Use the spatula to fold the egg in half, enclosing the spinach mixture, cilantro, and cheese inside.

6. Cook for about 20 seconds on each side, flipping the omelet over gently. When both sides are lightly golden, slide the omelet onto a plate. Cut in half for two people to share.

Tomato and Avocado Omelet *Serves 2*

2 Tbsp. Smart Balance Buttery Spread
¼ cup tomatoes, chopped
¼ cup Vidalia onion, finely chopped (see Appendix A, Tip #8)
1 tsp. minced garlic
2 Tbsp. scallions (green onions), thinly sliced

Veggie or sea salt and ground black pepper to taste
¾ cup egg whites
1 Tbsp. hemp milk
1 avocado, sliced (see Appendix A, Tip #6)
2 Tbsp. cilantro, chopped
2 slices rice pepperjack cheese

Directions

1. Coat medium skillet with cooking spray before heating over high heat. Add Smart Balance Buttery Spread, chopped tomatoes, onions, garlic, and scallions. Sauté for approximately 1–2 minutes. Season with salt and pepper to taste.

2. Pour vegetables into a colander to drain excess liquid. Set aside.

3. In a mixing bowl, whisk egg whites and milk.

4. Re-coat the skillet with cooking spray and heat over medium-high heat. Pour egg mixture into skillet and cook. Use a rubber spatula to lift the edge of the egg mixture as it cooks, and tilt the pan to allow any uncooked eggs to drain underneath the cooked portion.

5. When all egg mixture is cooked, fill the center of the omelet with the vegetable mixture, avocado, cilantro, and cheese. Use the spatula to fold the egg in half, enclosing the vegetable mixture, avocado, cilantro, and cheese.

6. Cook for about 20 seconds on each side, flipping the omelet over gently. When both sides are lightly golden, slide the omelet onto a plate.

7. Garnish with remaining cilantro. Cut in half for two people to share.

Goat Cheese and Zucchini Omelet *Serves 2*

2 Tbsp. Smart Balance Buttery Spread
1 tsp. minced garlic
½ cup zucchini, finely chopped
¼ cup red onion, chopped
  (see Appendix A, Tip #8)
¼ cup red bell pepper, finely sliced
  lengthwise
2 Tbsp. scallions (green onions), thinly
  sliced

Veggie or sea salt and ground black
  pepper to taste
¾ cup egg whites
1 Tbsp. hemp milk
¼ cup crumbled goat cheese
2 Tbsp. cilantro, chopped
1 tsp. chives, chopped

Directions

1. Coat medium skillet with cooking spray before heating over high heat. Add Smart Balance Buttery Spread, garlic, zucchini, onion, bell pepper, and scallions; sauté for approximately 2 minutes. Season with salt and pepper to taste.

2. Pour vegetables into a colander to drain excess liquid. Set aside.

3. In a mixing bowl, whisk egg whites and milk.

4. Re-coat the skillet with cooking spray and heat over medium-high heat. Pour egg mixture into skillet and cook. Use a rubber spatula to lift the edge of the egg mixture as it cooks, and tilt the pan to allow any uncooked eggs to drain underneath the cooked portion.

5. When all egg mixture is cooked, fill the center of the omelet with the vegetable mixture, adding the cheese, 1½ tablespoons of cilantro, and ½ teaspoon of chives. Use the spatula to fold the egg in half, enclosing the vegetable mixture, chives, cilantro, and cheese.

6. Cook for about 20 seconds on each side, flipping the omelet over gently. When both sides are lightly golden, slide the omelet onto a plate.

7. Garnish with remaining cilantro and chives. Cut in half for two people to share.

WHY GOAT CHEESE?

The most common reason for choosing goat cheese and other dairy products from goat's milk over the same products derived from cow's milk is that some people who have a sensitivity or allergy to cow's milk can drink goat's milk without any problems. You might have an allergy to cow's milk if you suffer from recurrent ear infections, asthma, eczema, and even rheumatoid arthritis. If so, replacing your cow-based dairy products with dairy items made from goat's milk may help to reduce some of the symptoms of these conditions.

Broccoli and Asparagus Omelet *Serves 2*

2 Tbsp. Smart Balance Buttery Spread
1 tsp. minced garlic
¼ cup broccoli florets
¼ cup asparagus tips, chopped
¼ cup red onion, chopped
    (see Appendix A, Tip #8)
¼ cup red bell pepper, finely sliced
    lengthwise

2 Tbsp. scallions (green onions), thinly
    sliced
Veggie or sea salt and ground black
    pepper to taste
¾ cup egg whites
1 Tbsp. hemp milk
¼ cup rice mozzarella cheese
2 Tbsp. cilantro, chopped
1 tsp. chives, chopped

Directions

1. Coat medium skillet with cooking spray before heating over high heat. Add Smart Balance Buttery Spread, garlic, broccoli, asparagus tips, onion, bell pepper, and scallions; sauté for approximately 1–2 minutes. Season with salt and pepper to taste.

2. Pour vegetables into a colander to drain excess liquid. Set aside.

3. In a mixing bowl, whisk egg whites and milk.

4. Re-coat the skillet with cooking spray and heat over medium-high heat. Pour egg mixture into skillet and cook. Use a rubber spatula to lift the edge of the egg mixture as it cooks, and tilt the pan to allow any uncooked eggs to drain underneath the cooked portion.

5. When all egg mixture is cooked, fill the center of the omelet with the vegetable mixture, adding cheese, ½ tablespoon of cilantro, and ½ teaspoon of chives. Use the spatula to fold the egg in half, enclosing the vegetable mixture, chives, cilantro, and cheese.

6. Cook for about 20 seconds on each side, flipping the omelet over gently. When both sides are lightly golden, slide the omelet onto a plate.

7. Garnish with remaining cilantro and chives. Cut in half for two people to share.

Vegetable Scrambled Eggs *Serves 2*

4 Tbsp. Smart Balance Buttery Spread
½ cup zucchini, finely chopped
¼ cup red onion, chopped
   (see Appendix A, Tip #8)
¼ cup red bell pepper, cut finely
   lengthwise
¼ cup tomatoes, diced
   (see Appendix A, Tip #7)
1Tbsp. scallions (green onions), thinly
   sliced

1Tbsp. cilantro, chopped
4 strips uncured, gluten-free turkey
   bacon (optional)
¾ cup egg whites
1 Tbsp. hemp milk
Veggie or sea salt and ground black
   pepper to taste
3–4 parsley sprigs

Directions

1. Coat medium skillet with cooking spray before heating over high heat. Add 2 tablespoons Smart Balance Buttery Spread, zucchini, onion, bell pepper, tomatoes, scallions, and cilantro. Sauté for approximately 2–3 minutes, then season with salt and pepper to taste.

2. Pour vegetables into a strainer to drain excess liquid. Set aside.

3. Re-coat skillet with cooking spray and heat over medium-high heat. Cook turkey bacon on either side until slightly crispy. Remove from heat and set aside on serving plate.

4. In a mixing bowl, whisk egg whites and milk. Add the vegetable ingredients to eggs and mix together. Season with salt and pepper to taste.

5. Add the remaining Smart Balance Buttery Spread to the skillet; heat over medium-high heat until melted. Pour egg mixture in skillet and cook. Using a rubber spatula, stir the egg mixture together until cooked, tilting the pan to allow any uncooked eggs to drain underneath the cooked portion.

6. Stir the egg mixture for another 20 seconds, then spoon onto the serving dish alongside the turkey bacon. Garnish with parsley sprigs.

QUICK TIPS

- This egg white scramble can be accomplished without any vegetables. Just add egg, milk, and dash of salt and pepper. Beat and mix and pour into skillet with 2 Tbsp. of Smart Balance Buttery Spread. Stir until cooked.
- We prefer Applegate Farms uncured gluten-free bacon because it is low in sodium and delicious.

Granny Smith Apple and Cheddar Cheese Omelet
Serves 2

¾ cup egg whites
1 Tbsp. hemp milk
Veggie or sea salt and ground black pepper to taste
2 Tbsp. Smart Balance Buttery Spread
½ cup Granny Smith apple, finely chopped
3 rice cheddar cheese slices
1 Tbsp. cilantro, chopped (optional)

Directions

1. In a mixing bowl, beat egg whites, milk, salt, and pepper together.

2. Spray medium skillet with cooking spray before heating over medium-high heat. Add Smart Balance Buttery Spread to the skillet.

3. Pour egg mixture in skillet and cook. Using a rubber spatula, stir the egg mixture together until cooked, tilting the pan to allow any uncooked eggs to drain underneath the cooked portion.

> ### Tips
> For those of you who like a little more tartness, you may use green apples instead of Granny Smith apples.
> The reason for using cheddar cheese as opposed to any other kind of cheese is the same reason why many people put a slice of cheddar cheese on top of a piece of apple pie: it is delicious!

4. When all egg mixture is cooked, fill the center of the omelet with the apples, cheese, and cilantro. Use the spatula to fold the egg in half, enclosing the apples, cilantro, and cheese.

5. Cook for about 20 seconds on each side, flipping the omelet over gently. When both sides are lightly golden, slide the omelet onto a plate. Cut in half for two people to share.

Healthy Waffles/Pancakes *Serves 2*

1 cup Arrowhead Mill Wild Rice Pancake
and Waffle Mix
1 egg (or egg substitute or egg whites)
1 Tbsp. olive oil
¾ cup hemp, rice, or soy milk

½ tsp. sea salt
Rice butter or Smart Balance Buttery
Spread (topping only)
Maple syrup
Fruit compote (optional, topping only)

Directions

1. Combine the pancake mix, egg, olive oil, milk, and salt. Mix until lumps disappear and batter is smooth. The batter must be thick.

2. **For waffles:** Heat waffle maker. Spray with cooking spray. Pour batter onto waffle maker and cook until golden brown and lightly crisp outside for approximately 3–4 minutes, depending on the baking time of the waffle maker.

   For pancakes: If cooking pancakes on the stovetop griddle, spray the griddle with cooking spray then preheat the griddle over medium-high heat. Using a measuring cup, measure less than ¼ cup batter to make a 4-inch pancake. Cook pancakes 1¼ minutes on each side or until surface bubbles and edges begin to dry before flipping on the other side to cook.

3. Serve hot topped with rice butter or Smart Balance Buttery Spread and 1 tablespoon of maple syrup.

4. Add favorite fruit or compote.

Ezekiel Cinnamon Raisin French Toast *Serves 4*

¾ cup egg whites
2 Tbsp. hemp milk
1 tsp. cinnamon
½ tsp. nutmeg
¼ tsp. vanilla extract

4 slices of Ezekiel 4:9 Cinnamon Raisin
   Bread
2 Tbsp. Smart Balance Buttery Spread
Pure maple syrup (or your favorite
   preserves)

Directions

1. In a bowl, whisk egg whites, milk, cinnamon, nutmeg, and vanilla extract until well blended.

2. Spray skillet with cooking spray and heat over medium-high heat. Cut bread slices in half diagonally and dip them in the egg mixture.

3. Place the dipped bread on hot skillet. Cook each side until golden brown, or approximately 30 seconds on each side.

4. Serve with Smart Balance Buttery Spread and warm maple syrup or preserves.

Chapter 9

Pasta Dishes

...and thus we came to Rome.
—Acts 28:14

Gluten-Free Spaghetti With Marinara *Serves 6*

½ cup olive oil
4 Tbsp. minced garlic
1 small sweet onion, chopped
(see Appendix A, Tip #8)
½ cup portobello mushrooms, sliced
½ cup cilantro, chopped
5–6 tomatoes, chopped
6–7 fresh basil leaves, chopped

Veggie or sea salt to taste
1 lb. ground tofu
2 Tbsp. maple syrup
1 lb. wheat- and gluten-free pasta,
quinoa, rice, or spelt pasta (choose
one type of pasta)
¾ cup rice Parmesan cheese
8 romaine lettuce leaves

Directions

1. In a pot or large saucepan, heat olive oil over high heat and add garlic, onion, mushrooms, cilantro, tomatoes, basil leaves, and salt. Cover and simmer for 10 minutes.

2. Add the tofu and 1 tablespoon of maple syrup; stir to reduce the acidity of the tomatoes. Simmer for about 30 more minutes.

3. Cook pasta according to package instructions.

4. Drain pasta and toss with a little olive oil to keep pasta loose. Transfer to serving bowl.

5. Pour sauce over pasta. Top with cheese.

6. Serve with a small romaine lettuce salad.

QUICK TIPS

- All pastas mentioned in this recipe are intended to be wheat and gluten free. Here are a few wheat- and gluten-free pastas that we enjoy on a regular basis: Mrs. Leeper's Corn Rotelli (www.mrsleepers.com); Lundberg's organic Spaghetti Brown Rice Pasta (www.lundberg.com); and brown rice penne, elbow, shells, and spirals by Tinkyada (www.tinkyada.com). Note: You can purchase these pastas at your local health food store or some local markets. Spelt, quinoa, millet, and rice are all great, but our favorite is Tinkyada Brown Rice Pasta. It is wheat and gluten free and certified kosher.
- Mom's Organic Traditional Pasta Sauce is one of our favorites (www.jelly.com). We use this sauce when pressed for time. However, we always enjoy making our own when we have the time.

Linguine With Basil and Tomatoes *Serves 6*

1 16-oz. package Tinkyada Linguine
4 large ripe tomatoes, chopped
3 Tbsp. kosher salt
½ cup olive oil
½ cup fresh basil, cut into strips
1–2 bay leaves
3 Tbsp. minced garlic
6–8 Tbsp. rice Parmesan cheese

Directions

1. Cook linguine according to package directions, being careful not to overcook. (Rice pasta quickly becomes mushy if overcooked.)

2. When cooked, drain linguine and rinse with cold water for a great texture. Transfer to serving bowl.

3. Add all other ingredients—tomatoes, salt, oil, basil, bay leaves, garlic, and cheese—and toss.

4. Remove bay leaves and serve.

WHAT IS TINKYADA LINGUINE?

Tinkyada is a Canadian company dedicated to making *wheat-free, gluten-free alternatives* to traditional wheat-based pasta. Their products are made from whole-grain rice and are certified organic and kosher. For more information, visit their website at www.tinkyada.com.

Penne With Roasted Tomatoes, Garlic, and Basil *Serves 6*

1 16-oz. package penne pasta
½ cup olive oil
4–6 Tbsp. minced garlic
2 cups roasted tomatoes, sliced
½ cup cilantro, chopped

½ cup basil, chopped
Veggie or sea salt and ground black
    pepper to taste
6–8 Tbsp. rice Parmesan cheese

Directions

1. Cook penne according to package directions. When cooked, drain and return to the pot.

2. In a saucepan, heat the olive oil over high heat. Add garlic, tomatoes, cilantro, ¼ cup basil, salt, and pepper. Cook for approximately 6–10 minutes.

3. Toss the ingredients into the penne pasta. Add the remaining fresh basil and top with cheese.

4. Serve hot or cold. If cold, refrigerate for 4 hours before serving.

Red Cabbage, Zucchini, and Rice Noodles *Serves 6*

3 Tbsp. olive oil
1 sweet onion, chopped (see Appendix A, Tip #8)
1 small red cabbage, shredded
Veggie or sea salt and ground black pepper to taste
1 lb. brown rice noodles

Directions

1. Heat oil in a pan over medium-high heat. Add onion and sauté for about 5 minutes.

> **Quick Tip**
>
> You can use the Teriyaki Sauce in chapter 5 to add another flavor to this dish.

2. Add the cabbage, salt, and pepper and cook over low heat for about 20 minutes.

3. In the meantime, cook your noodles according to package directions.

4. After draining noodles, add to pan with cabbage, mix well, and serve.

Wheat- and Gluten-Free Macaroni-n-Cheese *Serves 6*

1 16-oz. package quinoa or rice elbow macaroni
½ cup olive oil
1–2 Tbsp. soy, rice, or veggie margarine
Veggie or sea salt to taste

½ cup hemp, rice, or soy milk
½ cup Vegenaise (mayo substitute)
4–5 oz. rice mozzarella cheese
4–5 oz. rice cheddar cheese

Directions

1. Preheat oven to 350 degrees. Lightly coat baking dish with cooking spray and set aside. (If you want to skip baking, see the No-Bake Option below.)
2. Cook pasta according to package directions.
3. Drain pasta and return to pot on stove. Add olive oil, margarine, salt, milk, and Vegenaise.
4. Stir in both cheeses. (You can add more if you desire a cheesier dish.)
5. Transfer to baking dish. Add a little more cheese to top, and bake uncovered for about 10 minutes until top is slightly brown.

QUICK TIPS

This dish will become your kids' new favorite! This recipe works with any shape of spelt, quinoa, or rice pasta you can find—elbow macaroni, rotini (spirals), bowties, tubes, etc.

NO-BAKE OPTION

You can cook this on the stovetop instead of baking it in the oven. Just skip steps 1 and 5 above and cook the mixture from step 4 over medium heat for 10 minutes or until mixture is heated through and cheese is melted. Stir frequently to keep from sticking to the bottom of the pot.

Pasta and Fresh Veggies *Serves 6*

1 package spelt, quinoa, or rice pasta, wheat and gluten free
4–6 Tbsp. minced garlic
1 cup broccoli florets
½ cup fennel, chopped
½ cup bell pepper (any color), diced
2 yellow squashes, cubed
2 zucchini, cubed
½ cup scallions (green onions), chopped

4–6 tomatoes, chopped
1 sweet onion, chopped (see Appendix A, Tip #8)
½ cup olive oil
Veggie or sea salt and ground black pepper to taste
2 Tbsp. rice Parmesan cheese

Directions

1. Cook pasta according to package directions. After draining pasta, return it to the pot and set aside (on a cool surface).

2. Sauté garlic, broccoli, fennel, bell pepper, squash, zucchini, scallions, tomatoes, and onion in olive oil over medium-high heat; cover for approximately 3–5 minutes. Add salt and pepper to taste and mix well.

3. Pour sautéed veggies over pasta. Top with a sprinkle of rice Parmesan cheese.

4. Serve hot immediately, or cover and refrigerate for 4 hours to serve cold.

> **Quick Tip**
>
> This recipe works with any shape of gluten-free pasta you can find: spaghetti, linguine, rotini, penne, etc.

Spelt Lasagna *Serves 6*

1 16-oz. package spelt lasagna noodles
½ cup olive oil
6–8 tomatoes, chopped (or 1 jar spaghetti sauce)
4–6 Tbsp. minced garlic
¼ tsp. rosemary
1 lb. ground tofu
1 Tbsp. of maple syrup
1 tsp. dill

1 10-oz. package frozen chopped spinach
1 cup shiitake mushrooms, sliced (or any variety of mushrooms)
Veggie or sea salt and ground black pepper to taste
2 packages each of rice mozzarella and cheddar cheeses

Directions

1. Preheat oven to 350 degrees. Lightly coat baking dish with cooking spray and set aside.

2. Cook lasagna noodles according to package directions, being careful not to overcook. (Spelt becomes mushy when overcooked.)

3. Heat olive oil over high heat, then lower heat to medium. Add tomatoes, garlic, rosemary, tofu, maple syrup, and dill; sauté for approximately 2 minutes.

4. In a separate pan add ¼ cup water with 1 Tbsp. of salt. When it starts to boil, add the chopped spinach. Cover and simmer for approximately 5 minutes or until wilted. Then add mushrooms to the spinach; continue to cook until mushrooms become soft. Add salt and pepper to taste.

5. Layer in baking dish as you would regular lasagna. Suggested order of layers: pasta, tofu, spinach and mushrooms, cheese, and sauce. Repeat layers until all ingredients are used.

6. Bake for 35–45 minutes.

7. Serve with salad and garlic bread (See recipe for Ezekiel Garlic Bread in chapter 12.)

What Is Spelt?

Spelt contains a moderate amount of gluten. It is related to common wheat and is not suitable for people with celiac disease. However, some people with wheat allergy or wheat tolerance can tolerate spelt.

You can purchase spelt pasta at Whole Foods and other organic grocers. For more information, visit: www.whfoods.com.

Gluten-Free Macaroni Salad *Serves 6*

1 16-oz. package wheat- and gluten-free elbow macaroni
¾ cup Vegenaise (mayo substitute)
Veggie or sea salt and ground black pepper to taste
1 Tbsp. minced garlic
½ cup scallions (green onions), finely chopped
1½ tsp. prepared mustard

Directions

1. Cook pasta according to the package direction. When the pasta is cooked, drain and rinse with cold water.

2. Transfer macaroni to a large bowl. Add Vegenaise, salt, pepper, garlic, scallions, and prepared mustard. Mix well and season to taste.

3. Chill before serving (15–30 minutes).

TIPS

- Even though other types of pastas have been used to make different pasta dishes, we prefer the wheat- and gluten-free pastas. We like the consistency and the taste. The primary ingredients used as flour in wheat and gluten products are brown rice and corn. Spelt pasta is made with 100 percent spelt flour.
- The standard pastas are made of refined wheat flour. During the refining process, nutrients such as fibers, vitamins, minerals, and phytonutrients are stripped away, leaving a starchy and weak product.

Tri-Color Pasta With Broccoli and Carrots *Serves 6*

1 lb. tri-color spiral pasta, wheat and gluten free

3 Tbsp. olive oil

1 Tbsp. minced garlic

½ cup green bell pepper, sliced into strips

½ cup mushrooms, sliced

½ cup red onion, thinly cut on a diagonal (see Appendix A, Tip #8)

½ cup carrots, cut lengthwise

1 cup broccoli florets

1 Tbsp. Bragg Liquid Aminos

1 Tbsp. organic tamari sauce

Juice of 1 lemon

2 large tomatoes, cut into wedges

½ cup scallions (green onions), thinly sliced

Veggie or sea salt and ground black pepper to taste

Directions

1. Cook pasta according to package directions. Drain and transfer to serving bowl.

2. While pasta is cooking, add olive oil to saucepan over medium heat. Add garlic, bell pepper, mushrooms, onions, carrots, and broccoli florets. Sauté for 5–7 minutes and then remove from heat.

3. Transfer all sautéed ingredients to the macaroni bowl and blend. Stir in Bragg Liquid Aminos, tamari sauce, lemon juice, tomatoes, and scallions. Season with salt and pepper.

4. Can be refrigerated for 10 minutes and served cold or at room temperature.

Pasta Salad *Serves 6*

1 10-oz. package of rice pasta shells, wheat and gluten free

½ cup olive oil

3–4 Tbsp. minced garlic

1 cup fennel, finely sliced

2 red, green, or yellow bell peppers, cut in ½-inch cubes

1 large sweet onion, chopped or sliced (see Appendix A, Tip #8)

Veggie or sea salt and ground black pepper to taste

⅔ cup rice Parmesan cheese

½ cup cilantro

Directions

1. Cook pasta according to package directions. Drain and transfer to serving bowl.

2. In a saucepan over high heat, add olive oil, garlic, fennel, bell peppers, and onion. Stir until crisp-tender or fork-tender (see Appendix A, Tip #2). Season with salt and pepper, and spoon over pasta.

3. Top with cheese and cilantro and serve.

4. This dish can be put in the refrigerator and chilled for a few hours before serving, or it can be served warm. Either way it is delicious.

Pesto Bowtie Pasta With Asparagus *Serves 6*

1 16-oz. package of wheat- and gluten-free bowtie pasta

2–4 Tbsp. Easy Basil Pesto (see chapter 5)

½ cup olive oil

3 Tbsp. minced garlic

½ cup cilantro

½ cup scallions (green onions)

10 fresh asparagus spears, cut into ½-inch pieces

Veggie or sea salt and ground black pepper to taste

2 sprigs fresh basil

Directions

1. Cook pasta according to package directions. Drain and transfer to a serving bowl. Immediately add the pesto sauce to taste.

2. While pasta is cooking, in a saucepan heat the olive oil over high heat. Add garlic, cilantro, scallions, asparagus, salt, and pepper. Stir until slightly tender.

3. Pour the ingredients over the pasta. Mix well and garnish with fresh basil.

4. Season with salt and pepper.

Pasta Casserole *Serves 8*

1¾ cups penne pasta, wheat and gluten free (can also use brown rice, quinoa, or millet)

¼ green pepper, chopped

¼ cup black pimiento, diced

¼ cup hemp, rice, or soy milk

½ sweet onion, chopped (see Appendix A, Tip #8)

1 cup mushrooms, diced

½ tsp. sea salt or veggie salt

½ tsp. black pepper

3 Tbsp. minced garlic

1¾ cups rice cheese (yellow or mozzarella)

2 eggs (or egg substitute or egg whites)

½ cup Vegenaise (mayo substitute)

Directions

1. Preheat oven to 350 degrees.

2. Cook pasta according to package directions. Drain and transfer to a 2-quart casserole dish.

3. Combine remaining ingredients in a large bowl until well mixed. Pour over pasta in baking dish.

4. Bake for 45 minutes. Serve with a salad.

> ### Egg Substitute Recommendation
>
> We recommend Egg Replacer by Ener-G Foods. For more information, visit their website at www.ener-g.com.

Chapter 10

RICE DISHES

The fast is over—eat your fill!
—JOEL 2:19, THE MESSAGE

Black Rice With Cabbage *Serves 6*

1 lb. black and mahogany rice blend
½ cup black olives
¼ cup green olives
½ cup cocktail onions
½ cup raisins (golden or black, optional)
¼ cup olive oil
4 Tbsp. minced garlic
Veggie or sea salt and ground black
   pepper to taste
4 Tbsp. Smart Balance Buttery Spread

1 head cabbage, shredded
½ cup leek, thinly sliced
½ cup shredded carrots
½ cup scallions (green onions), thinly
   sliced

Directions

1. Cook rice according to package instructions.

2. Add black and green olives, cocktail onions, raisins, 1 tablespoon of olive oil, 1 tablespoon of garlic, salt, pepper, and 2 tablespoons of Smart Balance Buttery Spread. Stir and cover tightly. Set aside.

3. Heat remaining olive oil over high heat, and then add the cabbage, leek, carrots, and remaining garlic and Smart Balance Buttery Spread. Add salt and pepper to taste. Stir and cover over medium heat for approximately 10 minutes.

WHAT IS BLACK AND MAHOGANY RICE?

This rice blend is gluten free. It is juicy with a nutty-like flavor energized with sweet spices. This is a whole-grain brown rice blend of short-grain black rice and medium-grain mahogany rice originated from Japanese seeds. We recommend a gourmet field blend of black and mahogany rice by Lundberg called Black Japonica. For more information, visit the Lundberg website at www.lundberg.com.

BROWN RICE OPTION

Pour 2 cups of Uncle Ben's brown rice in pot with 2½ cups water, olive oil, and a pinch of salt. If you are preparing the rice in a rice cooker, add 2 cups water with the olive oil, a pinch of salt, 2–3 tablespoons of Browning & Seasoning Sauce; stir and cover tightly. (For further rice cooker instructions, see Appendix A, Tip #11.)

Rice and Kidney Beans *Serves 6*

2 cups Uncle Ben's rice
2 cups cold water
¼ cup olive oil
2–3 Tbsp. minced garlic
Veggie or sea salt and ground black pepper to taste
2 cans kidney beans (or pinto, black-eyed peas, or pigeon peas)
2 Tbsp. Smart Balance Buttery Spread

Directions

1. In rice cooker, place rice, water, olive oil, garlic, salt, pepper, and beans. Stir and cover. (For further rice cooker instructions, see Appendix A, Tip #11.)

2. When the rice is cooked, transfer to serving dish and top with Smart Balance Buttery Spread.

3. Serve alongside a main course dish.

OPTIONAL: WASH YOUR RICE

Some people prefer to wash rice before cooking. To wash your rice, simply pour uncooked rice into a bowl with cold water and stir it around. Remove any natural twigs or stones. Then pour the water out without losing any rice. (You use a very fine strainer). Then put it in the rice cooker.

Sautéed Veggies and Brown Rice *Serves 6*

4 Tbsp. olive oil

1 Vidalia onion, cut diagonally (see Appendix A, Tip #8)

2 shallots

4 Tbsp. minced garlic

1 bell pepper (any color), thinly sliced

½ cup fennel, thinly sliced

½ cup leek, thinly sliced

2 carrots, thinly sliced

Sea salt or veggie salt and ground black pepper to taste

3 zucchini, thinly sliced

2 cups broccoli florets

Any other veggies you desire

3 cups brown rice

Directions

1. In 2 tablespoons of olive oil over high heat, sauté the onion, shallots, 2 tablespoons of garlic, bell pepper, fennel, leek, carrots, salt, and pepper for about 5–7 minutes.

2. Remove from heat and cover for another 5 minutes.

> **RICE COOKER OPTION**
>
> If you have a rice cooker, you can use it to prepare the rice for this dish (see Appendix A, Tip #11).

3. In a separate pot, bring 1 cup cold water and salt, remaining olive oil, and remaining garlic to a boil. Add the zucchini to the boiling water for approximately 2–3 minutes. Use a slotted spoon to transfer zucchini to a large serving bowl, and set aside.

4. Let the garlic water boil again and add the broccoli for approximately 2–3 minutes or until the broccoli turns bright green. Drain and transfer to large serving bowl with zucchini. Repeat for any other veggies you desire.

5. Prepare brown rice according to package directions.

6. Pour the sautéed vegetables over the zucchini and broccoli and mix completely. Serve over rice.

Cook-Up Rice (West Indian Style) *Serves 6*

2 cups Uncle Ben's rice

2 Tbsp. browning sauce

¼ cup olive oil

½ cup carrots, diced

2 cans pigeon peas or green pigeon peas, washed and drained

¼ cup raisins

¾ cup coconut milk

½ tsp. of dried thyme (or 3–4 fresh sprigs)

1 Tbsp. of minced garlic

¼ cup caramelized pearl onions

Veggie or sea salt and ground black pepper to taste

½ cup scallions (green onions)

¼ cup olives, halved

Directions

1. In a rice cooker, place the rice and 2 cups water. (You can also make this dish on the stovetop by combining all ingredients and cooking until the rice is done.)

2. Add the browning sauce, olive oil, carrots, peas, raisins, coconut milk, thyme, garlic, pearl onions, salt, and pepper. Stir and cover tightly.

3. After 15 minutes, remove cover and add the scallions. Stir, cover, and let cook.

4. When the light goes off, the rice is cooked. Let it sit, covered, for another 20 minutes. (The steam will continue to cook everything.)

5. Then in a large bowl toss the rice mixture and olives.

6. Season with additional salt and pepper to taste.

> ### WHAT MAKES THIS RECIPE "WEST INDIAN STYLE"?
>
> The West Indian influence in this rice dish is the coconut milk added to the rice. It's also about everything cooking together. Cooking the main ingredients all together in your rice cooker is what makes it authentic West Indian style!

> ### BROWNING SAUCE SUGGESTION
>
> We use Kitchen Bouquet Browning & Seasoning Sauce for a variety of appearance effects. It contains a vegetable base of carrots, onions, celery, parsnips, turnips, salt, parsley, and spices along with a caramel color that enhances any dish—including this one. For more information, visit www.wegmans.com.

Yellow Rice *Serves 6*

2 cups Uncle Ben's rice
½ cup olive oil
1 tsp. saffron
1 cup green olives, halved
2 cups scallions (green onions), chopped
2 cups cilantro, chopped
1 red bell pepper, diced

1 small bag frozen green peas
3–6 Tbsp. Smart Balance Buttery Spread
1 cup green olives
Veggie or sea salt and ground black
    pepper to taste

Directions

1. In rice cooker, place rice, ¼ cup olive oil, 2 cups cold water, and saffron. Stir and then cover. (You can also prepare the rice on the stovetop if you don't have a rice cooker. Simply combine all ingredients in this step in a saucepan and cook according to the time designated on rice package.)

2. While rice is cooking, in a large bowl combine the olives, scallions, cilantro, and bell pepper. Set aside.

3. In a small saucepan boil 1 cup cold, salted water. Add the peas; remove from heat and let sit for 5 minutes uncovered. Drain and toss in the bowl with the other ingredients.

4. Stir rice to see if it is yellow enough. When rice is cooked, pour it into the large bowl and mix all ingredients.

5. Before serving, add the Smart Balance Buttery Spread and season with salt and pepper.

6. You may need to add the remaining olive oil for moisture.

Chapter 11

VEGAN SPECIALTIES

*I will never eat meat again, so that I will
not cause my brother to stumble.*
—1 CORINTHIANS 8:13

Vegan Ground Sausage *Serves 6*

¼ cup olive oil

2 Tbsp. minced garlic

½ lb. vegan ground sausage

½ cup celery, chopped

½ cup cilantro, chopped

2 Tbsp. chives

½ cup red bell pepper

1 onion, chopped

   (see Appendix A, Tip #8)

Veggie or sea salt and ground black

   pepper to taste

Directions

1. In a large skillet, heat olive oil over high heat. Add garlic and sausage and mix well.

2. Add the celery, cilantro, chives, bell pepper, and onion.

3. Season with salt and pepper to taste.

WORD OF CAUTION

We recommend a meatless sausage (vegan ground sausage) called Gimme Lean Sausage by Lightlife Foods, www.lightlife.com. However, if you have celiac disease, you should not consume this product because it contains some wheat and gluten.

Vegan Chicken Salad *Serves 6*

½ cup vegan chicken product
1 Tbsp. minced garlic
½ cup celery, finely chopped
¼ cup chives, finely chopped
1 small onion, chopped
   (see Appendix A, Tip #8)
¼ cup cilantro

¼ cup parsley
1 Tbsp. jalapeño pepper, chopped
2–3 Tbsp. Vegenaise (mayo substitute)
Veggie or sea salt and ground black
   pepper to taste
4–6 romaine lettuce leaves (optional)

Directions

1. Place the vegan chicken in a blender, chop, and transfer to a bowl.

2. Add garlic, celery, chives, onion, cilantro, parsley, jalapeño pepper, Vegenaise, salt, and pepper.

3. Serve with a romaine salad, or wrap the ingredients in whole lettuce leaves.

> ### WORD OF CAUTION
>
> For recipes requiring meatless chicken, we recommend vegan chicken products offered by Cedar Lake (www.cedarlakedirect.com or www.worthingtonfoods.com). Most health food stores, including your local grocery store's health food section, carry these products. However, if you have celiac disease, you cannot have this product because it contains some wheat and gluten.

Vegan Ground Beef Dish *Serves 6*

½ cup olive oil

2 Tbsp. minced garlic

2 cups vegan ground beef

½ cup celery, finely chopped

1 small onion, finely chopped (see Appendix A, Tip #8)

¼ cup cilantro, finely chopped

¼ cup chives, finely chopped

2 bay leaves

½ tsp. thyme

1 Tbsp. of lemon juice, squeezed

Veggie or sea salt and ground black pepper to taste

¼ cup parsley, finely chopped

Directions

1. In a large skillet, heat olive oil over high heat. Add garlic and ground beef; mix well.
2. Add the celery, onion, cilantro, chives, bay leaves, thyme, and lemon juice. Season with salt and pepper.
3. Garnish with parsley before serving.

WORD OF CAUTION

For recipes requiring meatless ground beef (vegan ground beef), we recommend Gimme Lean Beef by Lightlife (www.lightlife.com). However, if you have celiac disease you should not consume this product because it contains some wheat and gluten.

Vegan Scallop Salad *Serves 6*

1 cup Worthington Vegetable Skallops
1 Tbsp. minced garlic
½ cup celery, finely chopped
¼ cup chives, finely chopped
1 small onion, chopped
  (see Appendix A, Tip #8)
¼ cup cilantro

¼ cup parsley
1 Tbsp. jalapeño pepper, chopped
Juice of 1 lemon (or to taste)
2 Tbsp. Vegenaise (mayo substitute)
Veggie or sea salt and ground black
  pepper to taste

Directions

1. In a bowl combine the veggie scallops, garlic, celery, chives, onion, cilantro, parsley, jalapeño, lemon juice, and Vegenaise. Season with salt and pepper.

2. Mix well. Cover and chill for approximately 10 minutes, or serve at room temperature.

WORD OF CAUTION

We recommend Worthington & Loma Linda products (including their canned Vegetable Skallops) because they provide a variety of great vegetarian, vegan, and kosher food products. For more information, visit www.worthingtonfoods.com. However, if you have celiac disease, you cannot have this product, because it has some wheat and gluten.

Spelt Tacos *Serves 4*

1 package spelt tortillas
1 lb. ground tofu (made especially for
   spaghetti or tacos)
½ cup Spanish onion, finely chopped
   (see Appendix A, Tip #8)

½ cup cilantro, finely chopped
2–3 tomatoes, finely chopped
2 cups rice mozzarella cheese

Directions

1. Preheat oven to 350 degrees.

2. Heat up tortillas in the oven for about 7 minutes or until they are warm and flexible. (You can also microwave them by wrapping them in a wet paper towel, warming them for 20 seconds, turning them over, and microwaving them for 20 more seconds.) Transfer warm tortillas to a tortilla warmer or wrap them in a dishtowel and set aside.

3. Brown tofu with onion and cilantro in a skillet. (Reserve some onion and cilantro to put into your taco.)

4. To build a taco, spoon tofu in a line down the middle of a tortilla. Top with your choice of tomatoes, onion, cilantro, and cheese. (Don't spoon too much onto the tortilla, or it will be difficult to wrap.)

5. Wrap the tortilla around the line of fillers. You may wish to tuck in the ends of the tortilla as you wrap it.

> ### ADDITIONAL TOPPING IDEAS
>
> Spoon some organic tomato sauce on your taco, if desired. You might also try drizzling it with some warm olive oil.

> ### SPELT TORTILLAS
>
> Spelt tortillas can be hard to find. One chain that we know carries them is Whole Foods Markets. You can also visit www.foodforlife.com (makers of Ezekiel 4:9 Bread) for information on their wheat- and gluten-free tortillas and a store locator search based on your zip code. (Ezekiel tortillas will need to thaw out; they come frozen.)

Ezekiel Pizza *Serves 4*

3 tomatoes, chopped
½ cup cilantro
¼ cup basil
1 Vidalia onion, chopped (optional)
1 Tbsp. Easy Basil Pesto sauce
   (see chapter 5)
3 Tbsp. olive oil

Veggie or sea salt and ground black
   pepper to taste
4–6 pieces of Ezekiel 4:9 Bread
2 cups rice mozzarella cheese, shredded
4 Tbsp. rice Parmesan cheese

Directions

1. Combine tomatoes, cilantro, basil, onions, pesto sauce, and olive oil in a bowl. Season with salt and pepper to taste. Cover and marinate for about 30 minutes.

2. Preheat oven to 400 degrees.

3. Toast bread lightly. Spread bread with olive oil and top with mozzarella cheese. Place on baking sheet.

4. Spoon marinated tomato mixture on top of bread slices. (Don't overdo the toppings or your pizza will be soggy!) Top lightly with rice Parmesan cheese.

5. Bake in oven for 7 minutes or until lightly crispy.

> **QUICK TIPS**
>
> The kids love this one! For a "thin crust" pizza, use Ezekiel 4:9 tortillas instead of bread.

ADDITIONAL TOPPINGS

Traditional: ground tofu, onion, oregano, basil, rice mozzarella cheese, and rice Parmesan cheese

Spicy Italian: ground tofu, onion, green pepper, garlic, oregano, fennel, basil, crushed red pepper, rice mozzarella, and rice Parmesan cheese

Vegan Thai: natural peanut butter, grated ginger, lemon juice, tamari sauce, peanut oil, sesame oil, paprika, ground tofu, swiss chard, broccoli, and bean sprouts

Mexican: chopped tomato, sliced green onions, chopped green pepper, sliced chili peppers, sliced avocado, garlic, cumin, cilantro, canned corn, black beans, rice cheddar cheese, and rice mozzarella cheese

Greek: spinach, red bell pepper strips, sliced olives, crumbled herbed goat cheese

Mediterranean: capers, tofu cubes, sun-dried tomatoes, olives, and tarragon

California: broccoli, artichoke hearts, sliced black olives, sliced tomato, green and red bell pepper rings, rice Parmesan cheese

Mushroom Lovers: various mushrooms (oyster, cremini, chopped Portobello, etc.), shallots, Italian seasoning mix, rice Parmesan cheese, and rice Swiss cheese

Veggie Lovers: broccoli, cauliflower, bell peppers, onions, garlic, oregano, basil, fennel, rice mozzarella cheese, and rice Parmesan cheese

Ezekiel or Spelt Quesadillas *Serves 4*

4 Ezekiel tortillas (or spelt tortillas)
1 Tbsp. rice or soy margarine or Smart
    Balance Buttery Spread
4–6 slices of rice Monterey Jack or
    pepperjack cheese (or 2 cups rice
    mozzarella shredded cheese)
½ cup scallions (green onions), chopped
½ cup black olives, sliced

½ cup red onion, diced
    (see Appendix A, Tip #8)
½ cup tomatoes, diced
    (see Appendix A, Tip #7)
1 jalapeño pepper, chopped finely
Veggie or sea salt and ground black
    pepper to taste

Directions

1. Wrap tortillas in wet paper towel. (Ezekiel tortillas will need to thaw out; they come frozen.) Microwave on high for about 15 seconds, flip them over, and microwave for 15 more seconds. (Microwave cooking times vary, so be careful not to cook them too long. You don't want them to become rubbery.)

> **ADDITIONAL TOPPINGS**
>
> Try the following: green olives, feta cheese, goat cheese, sweet onion, chicken, shrimp, thinly cut beef, sausage, chopped spinach with mushrooms, or artichokes.

2. Spread one tortilla with margarine, top with cheese, and sprinkle with scallions, black olives, onions, tomatoes, and jalapeño pepper. Sprinkle with salt and pepper.

3. Spread margarine on second tortilla and place on top of the other tortilla. Then wrap in another wet paper towel and microwave for about 10–15 seconds on one side.

4. Use a pizza cutter to cut the quesadillas into wedge-shaped pieces (like a pie). Serve with fresh salsa or pico de gallo.

> **QUESADILLA MAKER OPTION**
>
> As an alternative to microwaving your quesadillas, try using a quesadilla maker. A quesadilla maker is similar in concept to a waffle iron. Simply plug it in, and when it's hot, layer your bottom tortilla, filler ingredients, and top tortilla, then close the lid. The machine will toast the tortillas, melt the cheese, and even leave scored lines to help you cut the quesadillas before serving. You can find quesadilla makers wherever small kitchen appliances are sold.

Brown Rice Tortilla Vegetable Wrap *Serves 6*

1 package of gluten-free tortillas
2–3 asparagus spears, chopped in
  ¾-inch pieces
¼ cup carrots, shredded
½ cup cucumbers, sliced
1 onion, chopped
  (see Appendix A, Tip #8)
¼ cup beets, shredded
¼ cup cilantro, finely chopped
¼ cup scallions (green onions), thinly
  sliced

1 ripe tomato, diced
  (see Appendix A, Tip #7)
½ cup bok choy (white portion)
2 Tbsp. tamari sauce
2 Tbsp. olive oil
Juice of 1 lemon
Veggie or sea salt and ground black
  pepper to taste
1 Tbsp. Vegenaise (mayo substitute)
2 romaine leaves

Directions

1. Place tortillas in a damp paper towel and microwave on high for no more than 30 seconds.

2. In a bowl combine the asparagus, carrots, cucumbers, onion, beets, cilantro, scallions, tomato, bok choy, tamari sauce, olive oil, lemon juice, salt, and pepper. Mix well.

3. Spread Vegenaise on the tortillas. Place the romaine leaves across the tortilla and top with asparagus mixture.

4. Wrap the tortillas and cut diagonally. Serve with a small salad.

Spinach Balls *Serves 6–8*

1 10-oz. package frozen chopped
   spinach, thawed
1 cup Ener-G Bread Crumbs
1 cup grated rice Parmesan cheese

Dash nutmeg
6 eggs (or egg substitute)
¾ cup Smart Balance Buttery Spread or
   rice butter

Directions

1. Preheat oven to 350 degrees.

2. Drain spinach and place on a paper
   towel. Draw up the sides of the paper
   towel around the spinach and wring
   the paper towel over the sink to
   squeeze any remaining water out of
   the spinach.

3. Mix all ingredients in a bowl. Shape
   into balls, place on a baking sheet, and flash freeze (see Appendix A, Tip #12).

4. Transfer frozen balls to greased baking
   sheet. Cook 20 minutes or until golden
   brown.

5. Drain on paper towel before serving.

> **FREEZE EXTRA
> SPINACH BALLS**
>
> Any unused spinach balls can
> be stored in the freezer (in
> freezer bags) for up to 4–6
> weeks.

Healthy Chile Rellenos With Beans *Serves 4–6*

10–15 Anaheim or Poblano chiles
   (peppers)
2 cups rice cheddar or mozzarella cheese
1 cup egg whites
2½ cups Ener-G Bread Crumbs or Italian

Seasoning Bread Crumbs
2–3 Tbsp. olive oil
1 15-oz. can pinto or black beans,
   drained and rinsed

Directions

1. Roast whole peppers either on a stovetop grill pan (see Appendix A, Tip #4), an outdoor grill, or in the broiler until dark brown but not black. Allow peppers to cool, but peel the skin off of the chiles while they are still relatively warm. Gently open up the peppers and remove the seeds.

2. Cut off the ends of the peppers and stuff them with cheese. Set aside.

3. Separate the egg whites over a shallow bowl or pie pan and whisk lightly. Pour bread crumbs in a second shallow bowl or pie pan.

4. Roll the peppers one by one in the egg whites and then dredge them in the bread crumbs.

5. Fry peppers in olive oil until slightly crispy brown.

6. Heat beans for 10–15 minutes. Serve with rellenos and garnish with cheese.

> ### ADDITIONAL SERVING IDEAS
>
> This dish can be served with yellow or brown rice, guacamole (chapter 3), blue tortilla chips, or cassava chips (a cassava is a root vegetable similar to a potato).

> ### WHAT ARE ANAHEIM AND POBLANO CHILES?
>
> Anaheim chiles are chili peppers named after the California city and have a sweet, mild flavor with just a hint of heat. They come in two colors—green or red—and have a long, narrow shape. Anaheim chiles are readily available in the United States and can be purchased fresh or canned.
>
> Poblano chile peppers originate in the state of Puebla, Mexico. They tend to have a mild flavor but can be extremely hot.

Broccoli and Spinach Quiche *Serves 6*

1 frozen 9-inch wheat- and gluten-free piecrust, thawed
½ cup broccoli florets
½ cup chopped spinach
½ cup scallions (green onions)
½ cup cilantro
½ cup sweet onion (such as Vidalia)
1 cup rice mozzarella cheese

Veggie or sea salt and ground black pepper to taste
3 tsp. Ener-G Egg Replacer (egg substitute)
4 Tbsp. water
½ cup Vegenaise (mayo substitute)
½ cup hemp, rice, or soy milk

Directions

1. After thawing the piecrust, form the crust in a pie pan and pierce with a fork.

2. Preheat oven to 350 degrees.

3. In a large bowl, mix the broccoli florets, spinach, scallions, cilantro, onion, cheese, salt, and pepper. Spoon the ingredients into the piecrust.

4. In a separate bowl mix Egg Replacer and water thoroughly before adding Vegenaise and milk. Mix well and pour the over the ingredients in the piecrust.

5. Bake for approximately 30–45 minutes or until golden brown.

SERVING TIPS

- Add your favorite meat to the quiche (i.e., shrimp, tuna, turkey bacon, etc.).
- Egg Replacer by Ener-G is an egg substitute we recommend. It is wheat, gluten, and nut free as well as cholesterol free, and it contains no preservatives, artificial flavorings, or sugar. This product can be purchased from your local health food supermarket. The instructions provide you with information to assist in determining equivalency to whole eggs.
- As an alternative, you can skip the egg substitute and use egg whites or just two eggs instead.
- Many people find that the gluten-free piecrust makes them feel less bloated than regular piecrust.

Hoppin' John (Vegan Style) *Serves 6*

1 cup brown rice
¼ cup olive oil
1 15-oz. can black-eyed peas
2–3 Tbsp. minced garlic
1 Tbsp. jalapeño pepper
1 tomato, diced (see Appendix A, Tip #7)
1 red onion, sliced diagonally
   (see Appendix A, Tip #8)

1 cup cilantro, chopped
1 cup scallions (green onions), chopped
½ tsp. thyme
2–3 Tbsp. Smart Balance Omega-3
   Buttery Spread
Veggie or sea salt and ground black
   pepper to taste

Directions

1. In a rice cooker or on the stovetop, combine rice with 1 cup of water. Add olive oil to the rice and stir.

2. Add black-eyed peas, garlic, jalapeño pepper, tomato, onion, ½ cup cilantro, ½ cup scallions, thyme, Smart Balance, salt, and pepper.

> **WHAT IS HOPPIN' JOHN?**
>
> Hoppin' John is traditionally made of black-eyed peas, rice, and pork. It is a Southern US variation of a Caribbean rice and beans dish.

3. Stir, cover tightly, and simmer. Check once or twice and stir and taste to see if rice is seasoned. With the rice cooker, when the rice is cooked it automatically turns itself off. However, if cooking on the stovetop, it will take approximately 20 minutes.

4. Garnish with remaining scallions and cilantro. Add salt and pepper to taste, and serve.

> **HOW TO ADD SMOKY FLAVOR TO MEATLESS DISHES**
>
> There is a product called Liquid Smoke that will give your meatless dishes a smoky flavor normally given off by the meat. For further information, see www.colgin.com.

Fried Cucumbers   *Serves 6*

2 large English or regular cucumbers,
   peeled and cut lengthwise
½ cup olive oil

Veggie or sea salt and ground black
   pepper to taste
¾ cup egg whites, lightly beaten
1 cup Ener-G Bread Crumbs

Directions

1. Coat the cucumbers with 2 Tbsp. of olive oil, and season with salt and pepper.

2. Dip the cucumbers in the egg whites and place them in a plastic bag with the bread crumbs. Shake until cucumbers are thoroughly covered with bread crumbs.

3. Heat remaining olive oil in a skillet over high heat. Place the cucumbers into the hot oil and fry on both sides until golden brown.

4. Place on paper towel to absorb excess oil before serving.

Fried Green Beans   *Serves 6*

1 lb. fresh green beans
Juice of 1 lemon
2 Tbsp. minced garlic
½ cup olive oil

Veggie or sea salt and ground black
   pepper to taste
¾ cup egg whites, lightly beaten
1 cup Ener-G Bread Crumbs

Directions

1. Season the green beans with lemon juice, garlic, 2 Tbsp. of olive oil, and salt and pepper to taste.

2. Then dip the green beans in the egg whites. Place 10–15 beans at a time in a plastic bag with the bread crumbs and shake until green beans are thoroughly covered with bread crumbs.

3. Heat remaining olive oil in a skillet over high heat. Place the green beans into the hot oil and fry on both sides until golden brown.

4. Place on paper towel to absorb extra oil before serving.

Braised Sweet Fennel *Serves 4*

2 large bulbs fennel, chopped
2 vegetable bouillon cubes
3 Tbsp. olive oil
1 Tbsp. wheat- and gluten-free organic millet flour
Veggie or sea salt to taste

Directions

1. While you are chopping the fennel bulbs, chop 2 tablespoons of the leaves for a garnish and set the leaves aside.

2. In a skillet bring 1¾ cups water and bouillon cubes to a boil with the fennel bulbs.

3. Reduce heat to low, cover, and simmer for about 15 minutes or until fennel is tender.

4. Using a slotted turner, transfer fennel to a serving dish, cover, and keep warm.

5. Return the empty skillet to the stove. Over medium heat whisk olive oil and flour in the skillet until smooth. Continue stirring until the mixture is slightly thickened and boils. Add salt and pepper.

6. Spoon sauce over the fennel, and garnish with chopped fennel leaves before serving.

Green Beans *Serves 4*

3 Tbsp. minced garlic
1 lb. fresh green beans
4 Tbsp. Smart Balance Buttery Spread
Juice of 1 lemon
1 tsp. thyme
Veggie or sea salt and ground black pepper to taste

Directions

1. Boil 3 cups of cold, salted water, with 1 tablespoon of minced garlic added.

2. When water has come to a boil, add the green beans and blanch for approximately 2 minutes, then promptly remove and place in a large bowl.

3. Melt Smart Balance in a glass bowl in the microwave on high for about 30 seconds or until the Smart Balance spread is liquefied. Then add the lemon juice, thyme, and remaining garlic to the bowl. Blend all together and set aside.

4. Pour the butter mixture over the green beans, season with salt and pepper, and mix until the green beans are thoroughly coated.

> ### QUICK TIP
>
> Add toasted slivered almonds to the butter mixture for extra health-boosting benefits.

Chapter 12

BREADS

I am the bread of life.
—JOHN 6:48

AS YOU READ at the beginning of this cookbook, when you are on a Daniel fast, you need to stay away from wheat and gluten products. This includes any kind of white flour product such as bread, pasta (even whole wheat), muffins, bagels, tortillas, etc. However, you may eat Ezekiel 4:9 Bread or Essene bread.

Ezekiel 4:9 Organic Sprouted Whole-Grain Products are inspired by the Bible: "Take thou also unto thee wheat, and barley, and beans, and lentiles, and millet, and fitches [spelt], and put them in one vessel and make thee bread of thereof" (Ezekiel 4:9, KJV). This bread is flourless, organic, complete protein, and sprouted whole grain. The protein closely parallels the protein found in milk and eggs. Sprouting neutralizes phytic acid—a substance present in grains that inhibits absorption of nutrients. Sprouting neutralizes or "predigests" grains through enzymatic activities to promote digestibility of the grain. For further information, see www.foodforlife.com.

Likewise, Essene bread, so named for the ancient Judaic sect known as the Essenes, is also sprouted from grain, berries, and water. Both breads are permissible on the Daniel fast. However, if you suffer from celiac disease, you are encouraged not to eat any bread that is not wheat and gluten free.

Ezekiel or Millet Toast *Serves 2*

4 slices Ezekiel 4:9 Bread or millet bread
4 tsp. rice or soy margarine or Smart Balance
    Buttery Spread
4 tsp. Polaner's All Fruit spread (optional)
4 tsp. almond butter (optional)
4 tsp. honey (optional)

> ### QUICK TIP
>
> Ezekiel 4:9 Bread comes in a variety of flavors, including cinnamon raisin. Choose your favorite. See www.foodforlife.com.

Directions

1. Toast Ezekiel 4:9 Bread or millet bread on medium (not too lightly and not too charred).

2. Spread toast with margarine and top with fruit spread, almond butter, or honey.

Ezekiel Grilled Cheese *Serves 2*

4 slices Ezekiel 4:9 Bread
4 tsp. Smart Balance Buttery Spread
4 slices of rice cheddar or pepperjack cheese
1 beefsteak tomato, sliced (or tomato soup)

> ### ADDITIONAL TOPPINGS
>
> In addition to the cheese, you can add turkey bacon, sliced avocados, and sliced red onion. Kids really like this sandwich.

Directions

1. Heat skillet over high heat and coat with cooking spray.

2. Butter the bread on both sides. Put cheese between the slices of bread. Place in skillet and gently press down with a spatula during grilling.

3. When one side is golden, turn the sandwich over and brown on the other side.

4. Cut in half and serve with tomato slices or a cup of tomato soup.

> ### RECOMMENDED CHEESE
>
> The cheese we use during the fast and afterward is by Galaxy Nutritional Foods. They have three different flavors, slices and shredded, and the taste is delicious. We also find the consistency is more like dairy cheese, and it melts well. For further information, see www.galaxyfoods.com.

Ezekiel Garlic Bread   *Serves 8*

8 slices Ezekiel 4:9 Bread

3 Tbsp. rice or soy margarine

2 Tbsp. minced garlic

Directions

1. Preheat oven to 450.

2. Coat a baking sheet with cooking spray. Spread margarine on both sides of bread and place on baking sheet.

3. Brush or spoon garlic on each slice of the bread until evenly distributed.

4. Bake until golden brown, approximately 7 minutes on each side.

ADDITIONAL TOPPINGS AND TIPS

- **Cheese:** You can sprinkle rice Parmesan cheese on each side of the bread just before baking. We prefer it with a little rice mozzarella cheese instead. When we use the mozzarella cheese, we only put it on one side of the Ezekiel 4:9 Bread.
- **Pesto:** If you like pesto, it's another great way to spice up the Ezekiel 4:9 Bread. (See our Easy Basil Pesto recipe in chapter 5.) Follow the directions above, but instead of using rice or soy margarine, use the pesto sauce (only on one side). Then place 2 slices of tomato on it. Cover it with 2–3 tablespoons of rice mozzarella cheese. Then add 2–3 leaves of fresh basil. Bake until the cheese melts or for approximately 10 minutes.
- **Toaster Oven:** We often use the toaster oven for bread dishes instead of the oven. If the oven is already hot because of something else on the menu, we will use it for the bread too; otherwise, we use the toaster oven instead.

Essene Bread *Makes 2 loaves*

This recipe requires a few days of prep time for the wheat berries to sprout, so be patient!

3 cups wheat berries

Directions

> **QUICK TIP**
>
> You can occasionally spray the loaves with water during baking (or place a shallow pan of water on a lower oven rack) to keep them from drying out.

1. Rinse the wheat berries in cool water, drain, and place in a large bowl or sprouting jar. Add enough cool water to cover the berries. Cover the bowl or sprouting jar, and let soak at room temperature overnight, or for about 12 hours.

2. Drain the berries, and for the next few days, rinse the berries 2–3 times a day, cover them, and return them to the dark. They will begin to sprout.

3. When the sprouts reach about ¼ inch in length (after about 3 days), skip the last rinse and instead grind them in a coffee grinder, food mill, or food processor.

4. Transfer the ground grain onto a cutting board and knead the grain for about 10 minutes.

5. Wet your hands and form the dough into two small loaves.

6. Preheat oven to 250 degrees. Coat a baking sheet with cooking spray (or olive oil). Transfer the loaves onto the baking sheet and bake for about 2½ hours.

7. Remove from oven, cool loaves on racks and store in the refrigerator for up to 4 weeks or freeze.

> **QUICK FACTS ABOUT ESSENE BREAD**
>
> Essene is a sprouted-grain bread. It is one of the simplest, most nutritious, and oldest breads in the world. An ancient recipe for this bread can be found in a first-century manuscript called *The Essene Gospel of Peace*, which is where the bread gets its name.

Appendix A

Tips and Techniques

Tip #1: How to Remove Seeds and Rind From Pumpkin or Calabaza Squash

It is our experience that the calabaza squash is often cut in quarters or halves by the grocer. If you can only find whole calabazas or pumpkins in your store, ask the produce manager to halve or quarter it for you, or just cut it in half or quarters when you get home.

To remove the seeds and rind, wash the calabaza pieces and remove the seeds with a spoon, and then boil the pieces (with the rind still on). This makes it easier to remove the rind.

If you buy more calabaza or pumpkin than you need for a specific recipe, use it as a garnish or select one of the other recipes from this book that also use pumpkin/calabaza.

Tip #2: How Do You Know If It's Tender Enough?

Throughout this book when we say "fork-tender," we want you to test the tenderness of the food by poking it with a fork. If the fork easily penetrates, then it is cooked.

Tip #3: Using Fresh Beets

If you opt to use fresh beets for our Sweet Potato Salad recipe, we recommend that you boil 1–2 beets in 4 cups salted water until fork-tender. Rinse under cold water. Remove the skins and dice beets. You may want to use gloves when removing the skins and dicing the beets so your hands do not get stained.

Tip #4: Don't Have a Grill Pan? Here's an Option!

Several of our recipes call for a grill pan, but we also recommend using any of the George Foreman grills. We often prepare dishes using a George Foreman grill because it is easy to use and clean. In addition, it cooks on both sides and drains off fat, making it almost impossible to burn foods. Note: We prefer the grill that has a temperature gauge. For more information, visit www.georgeforemancooking.com.

Tip #5: How to Use a Salad Spinner

A salad spinner, which you can usually find wherever kitchen products are sold, allows you to dry lettuce relatively quickly and easily. You put the washed lettuce in a sieve that fits inside a bowl, and cover it with a lid. A pump-like mechanism in the lid allows you to spin the sieve around very quickly inside the bowl, effectively spinning all the water off of the lettuce and leaving it in the bowl when you remove the sieve.

Tip #6: Cutting and Slicing Avocados

To remove an avocado from its skin, start by cutting all the way around the avocado lengthwise and twisting it in half to expose the stone (seed) in one half. Remove the stone with a spoon or by gently tapping the sharp edge of the knife into the stone until it sticks in the stone, and then turning the knife to twist and release the stone. (If you use the knife method, you might want to hold the avocado in a folded dishtowel to protect the palm of your hand from the knife blade as you tap it into the stone.)

Now that you've halved the avocado and removed the stone, the next step is to remove the meat from the skin. If you're making guacamole, it doesn't really matter if you just scoop out the meat of an avocado with a spoon to remove it from the skin. After all, you're just going to mash it up! But some recipes call for avocado slices. In those cases, you want to keep the meat intact, and the scooping method can make this a challenge.

For easy avocado slices, try cutting the slices *before* you separate the meat from the skin. Here's how: Set the avocado halves, meat side up, on the counter and use a knife to cut the inside of the avocado halves into long slices (about the width of an orange section). It's fine to slice through the avocado skin right along with the meat when you do this. Then you should be able to separate the avocado slices from the skin pretty easily with your fingers.

This method should produce avocado slices that are about the same shape and size as apple slices.

TIP #7: HOW TO SEED AND DICE A TOMATO

1. Place the tomato stem side up on a cutting board. Using a sharp, serrated knife, start your cut next to the stem and slice downward in a C shape to cut the flesh away from the seeds.

2. Repeat, cutting several tomato "petals" until all the flesh has been removed from the pocket of seeds in the center.

3. Discard the stem and seeds. If there are remaining seeds or white areas on the tomato petals, scrape them off with a knife and discard.

4. Gently push down on the first petal to flatten it somewhat. Slice the tomato into strips that are about half an inch wide. Hold the strips together and slice across them every half an inch. Repeat for each tomato petal.

TIP #8: TRICK TO CUTTING ROUND VEGETABLES

For more stability when cutting rounded vegetables such as onions, you can slice a thin sliver off of the bottom of the vegetable first. Set the vegetable on a flat surface while cutting.

TIP #9: HOW TO PREPARE PAPAYA

Start by cutting the papaya in half, and then hold it over a trashcan and spoon out the seeds right into the trash. Now you can go a few different ways, depending on the shape you need for your recipe.

- **Balled**—No need to peel the papaya for this method. You simply use a melon baller or small ice cream scooper to scoop out balls of papaya flesh for desserts or fruit salads.
- **Sliced or cubed**—If you need to have slices or chunks of papaya, the next step is to cut away the peel with a sharp knife or vegetable peeler. Then simply cut the peeled papaya halves into slices or chunks.
- **Shredded**—For shredded papaya, after seeding the papaya, the next step is to cut away the peel with a sharp knife or vegetable peeler. Then simply shred the peeled papaya halves with a vegetable shredder.

TIP #10: HOW TO SEED A CUCUMBER

If the cucumber is not organic, then you should peel the skin. The reason for that is because cucumbers are usually waxed and you don't want to eat the waxed skin. Cut cucumber in half lengthwise. Scoop out the seeds with a small spoon and discard. Put the halves back together and cut lengthwise down the center and dice.

TIP #11: USING A RICE COOKER

For most of the recipes in this book that include rice, you can opt to use a rice cooker instead of the stovetop cooking method. Follow your manufacturer's directions, or use these basic guidelines for cooking rice in your rice cooker:

1. Place equal amounts of rice and water in the cooker. (You can also add garlic, olive oil, beans, and other ingredients at this time if the recipe calls for it.)

2. Stir, cover, and start the cooker.

3. After the cooker is finished, it will automatically turn off. Let the rice sit for another 5 minutes (or longer if the recipe calls for more time).

4. Toss the rice into a serving bowl. If serving it plain, you can add some Smart Balance Buttery Spread and season with salt and pepper before serving.

TIP #12: HOW TO FLASH FREEZE

Flash freezing often refers to freezing a food at extremely cold temperatures, well below freezing, as soon as possible after harvesting, butchering, or catching it in order to preserve as many nutrients as possible. Home cooks generally lack the resources needed for real flash freezing. But the term can also refer to a technique that involves freezing food items individually, such as spinach balls, meatballs, hamburger patties, chicken nuggets, french toast, waffles, small loaves of bread, pre-made cookie dough, etc.

To flash freeze, simply lay out the individual pieces of food on a baking sheet, cover with plastic wrap, and place the sheet in your freezer. Once the food is frozen, either use it in a recipe immediately or transfer it to freezer bags or plastic containers for long-term freezer storage.

Quick Glance Shopping List for the Daniel Fast

Legumes
Split peas, sweet green peas, sweet green peas, lentils (brown, green or red)

Beans
Garbanzo, pinto, kidney, black, lima, cannellini, navy, low-fat refried beans, green soy beans, hummus, split peas (yellow or green)

Nuts and seeds
Almonds, hazelnuts, whole nuts, walnuts, pecan halves, peanuts, pistachios, sunflower seeds, pumpkin seeds, sesame seeds

Vegetables
Asparagus, artichokes, bamboo shoots, bean sprouts, beets, bell or other peppers, broccoli, brussels sprouts, cauliflower, celery, chives, onion, leeks, garlic, cucumber, cabbage, eggplant, green beans, mushrooms, radishes, snow peas, fennel bulb

Lettuce/mixed greens
Romaine, red and green leaf lettuce, endive, spinach, arugula, radicchio, watercress, chicory, bok choy, escarole, Swiss chard, kale, collard greens, spinach, dandelion greens, mustard or beet greens, fennel leaves, endive, escarole

Squash
Spaghetti squash, winter squash, zucchini, acorn or butternut, pumpkin/calabaza

Fruit
Apples, apricots, blackberries, blueberries, raspberries, strawberries, cherries, fresh figs, grapes, grapefruit, honeydew melon, nectarine, oranges, peaches, pears, plums, tangerines
Whole grains
Amaranth; barley; quinoa,; Texmati, Basmati or other brown rice; buckwheat; millet; Grape-Nuts; whole oats; spelt; kamut
Pastas
Brown rice pasta, corn, quinoa, spelt, and kosher-certified, wheat- and gluten-free pastas (see Gluten-Free Spaghetti With Marinara recipe in chapter 9 for our brand-name recommendations for wheat- and gluten-free pastas)
Condiments
Cinnamon, mustard, tamari soy sauce, lime, lemon, flavored extracts, soy butter, Vegenaise, flaxseed oil, extra-virgin olive oil, Old Bay Seasoning, fresh basil, cilantro, cumin, ginger, lemon juice, oregano, parsley, chive, green onions, organic minced garlic, garlic, pepper (by Baron Specialty Foods), and spices and herbs of your choice
Protein
Tempeh, block tofu (fresh or baked), rice, soy or veggie cheese, ground tofu
Dairy
Hemp, almond, rice, soy or soy/rice milk

Daniel Fast Sample Menu

T HE OBJECT OF the Daniel fast is to spend time in contemplative meditation with the Lord. You don't want to be distracted with what to eat. But some of us may have a medical condition that warrants us to eat and take medicine, or some are in stressful jobs. The objective is to spend time in prayer with Jesus.

This is just a sample day's menu. If you can do without the food portion of the snacks and just have the beverages, then do so. Use that time to spend time with the Lord. If you can eat one meal a day, then by all means do so. You have to do what is right for you.

The fast is between you and the Lord. He will show you. There is no condemnation for those in Christ Jesus. If the sample plan works for you, then by all means adopt it as yours.

We have had friends who did not enjoy fasting because it became a burden. We don't believe that God wants us to find fasting a burden. That is one of the reasons we feel the Lord has given us all of these various ways of preparing veggies and fruits while participating in a partial fast.

The last thing to consider is to prepare ahead. You can prepare a pot of soup to last a whole week or prepare several salads or any of the recipes in this book ahead of time and have them ready so that your whole week is not consumed with thoughts of "What am I going to eat?" Plan and prepare ahead so that your time during the fast is wonderful and you can focus on the Lord.

Upon waking
8–16 ounces of room temperature or warm water with lemon. (If you are drinking from a 16.9-oz. bottle of water, then you need to drink no less than five bottles of water per day.)

Breakfast
The equivalent of 2 cups of your choice of fruit: apple, pear, strawberries, blueberries, banana, grapefruit, watermelon, cantaloupe, apricot, plums, prunes, etc.
Hot beverage, green tea, or water with lemon

Midmorning snack (optional)
The equivalent of 2 cups of your choice of fruit: apple, pear, strawberries, blueberries, banana, grapefruit, watermelon, cantaloupe, apricot, plums, prunes, etc.
Hot beverage, green tea, or water with lemon

Lunch
2 stalks of celery with hummus (see chapter 3)
1 cup of your choice of soup (see chapter 4)

Midafternoon snack (optional)
A handful of walnuts
Hot beverage, green tea, or water with lemon

Dinner
1 serving of your choice of main course/cooked side (see chapter 2) or raw side/salad (see chapter 3)
Hot beverage, green tea, or water with lemon

Evening snack (optional)
1 handful of your choice of snack (see chapter 7)
Hot beverage, green tea, or water with lemon

SAMPLE MENU FOR LIFE AFTER THE FAST

THE OBJECTIVE OF healthy eating after the fast is to aid in your lifestyle change. You can eat almost anything, but it must be done in moderation. Please stay away from fast foods or heavy fried foods. Remember that you are the temple of the living God (2 Cor. 6:16).

Prepare your food in advance, so if pressed for time you won't just grab anything. Planning is essential when planning a healthy lifestyle change.

Consider joining a gym. If this is not possible, take a daily walk around your community or during lunch breaks at work. Speaking of work, take your lunch to work as often as possible. When you do have to go out for lunch, choose wisely.

You can enjoy 3 cups mixed green vegetables or salads with protein. Try to choose the low carbohydrate vegetables, such as zucchini and mushrooms, with 6 ounces of protein. Eat lots of fresh salads, but be mindful of your salad dressing choices.

Upon waking
8–16 ounces of room temperature or warm water with lemon. (If you are drinking from a 16.9-oz. bottle of water, then you need to drink no less than five bottles of water per day.)
Breakfast
Your choice of omelet (see chapter 8)
Your choice of fruit (half of a cantaloupe, a whole grapefruit, or whole pear)
Herbal tea (see chapter 6)
Midmorning snack (optional)
Pumpkin and Carob Mix (see chapter 7)
Lunch
Your choice of soup (see chapter 4) or salad (see chapter 3)
Hot beverage, green tea, or water with lemon
Dinner
Stir-Fried Vegetables (see chapter 2)
Your choice of a main course/cooked side (see chapter 2), rice dish (see chapter 10), or vegan (meatless) dish (see chapter 11)
Your choice of salad (see chapter 3) with dressing (see chapter 5)
Hot beverage, green tea, or water with lemon

About the Authors

Originally from Los Angeles, Pastor John Cavazos, a classically trained singer, dancer, actor, and pianist, began his career on Broadway as a performer before becoming the minister of music at his church in New York City, where he met his wife, Ann Marie Cavazos, a native of Trinidad and Tobago. As a vocal coach and teacher in demand in the Orlando area, John regularly performs with the Voices of Liberty at Epcot and is an adjunct music professor at Rollins College.

Ann Marie earned her juris doctor (JD) from Temple University School of Law and her BS from John Jay College of Criminal Justice. She is a law professor at Florida Agricultural and Mechanical University (FAMU) College of Law in Orlando, Florida, and the director of the legal clinic and pro bono programs.

Together they have two beautiful and accomplished daughters—Ariel, age twenty, a junior at Troy University, and Jerusha, age eighteen, a freshman at the University of Central Florida (UCF).

Formerly John and Ann Marie served for eight years with Dr. Mark Chironna and are now the copastors of a brand-new thriving congregation, Christ the King Church in the South Orlando area. The mandate they have received from God, "Teach My people how to live for Christ," includes learning how to eat right! They are a three-streams, one-river congregation. Visit their website at www.christtheking3streams.com.

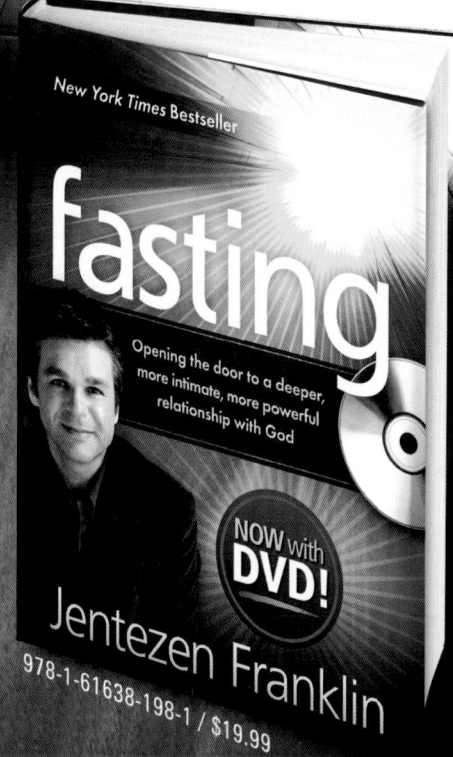